SACRIFICE: ITS NATURE
AND FUNCTION

SACRIFICE: ITS NATURE AND FUNCTION

Henri Hubert
and Marcel Mauss

Translated by
W. D. Halls

Foreword by
E. E. Evans-Pritchard

THE UNIVERSITY OF CHICAGO PRESS

© 1964 by E. E. Evans-Pritchard
Published 1964
Midway reprint 1981
Printed in the United States of America

ISBN: 0-226-35679-5
LCN: 64-12260

CONTENTS

FOREWORD

by E. E. Evans-Pritchard

SOME YEARS AGO my colleagues and I at Oxford came
to the conclusion that some of the more important essays
of the school of the *Année sociologique* should be published in English translations and so reach a wider public.
Several volumes have already been published,[1] and the
series has, I think, served the purpose for which it was
intended. We have therefore been encouraged to add to
the volumes already in print.

Hubert and Mauss' Essay on Sacrifice is one of the gems
of the *Année,* and it treats of a subject of the utmost importance and one central in the study of comparative
religion. Robertson Smith was undoubtedly right, even if
his attempts at evolutionary reconstruction were vitiated
by errors and misconceptions, in claiming that the *sacrificium* is the basic rite in ancient (and primitive) religion,
and also in saying that since sacrifice is so general an

[1] Emile Durkheim, *Sociology and Philosophy,* trans. by D. F.
Pocock with an introduction by J. G. Peristiany, 1953; Marcel
Mauss, *The Gift,* trans. by Ian Cunnision with an introduction by
E. E. Evans-Pritchard, 1954; Robert Hertz, *Death and the Right
Hand,* trans. by Rodney and Claudia Needham, with an introduc-
tion by E. E. Evans-Pritchard, 1960; Emile Durkheim and Marcel
Mauss, *Primitive Classification,* trans., edited, and with an intro-
duction by Rodney Needham, 1963. The previous volumes were
published by the same publishers as the present one: Cohen and
West.

institution we must seek for a general meaning of it in some general explanation.

The literature on sacrifice is enormous, but the sociological and social-anthropological contributions to it have been few. This is certainly one of the most important of them. I find its conclusions, evidently influenced by Robertson Smith's idea of the Semitic gods being reflections, symbols, of the mystical unity of social groups, rather lame, but as a study of the structure, or one might almost say the grammar, of the sacrificial rite the Essay is superb. Though I am unable to comment on what the authors say about the details of Vedic and Hebrew sacrifices, what they say about them is intended to have general application to all sacrificial acts—or at any rate all blood sacrifices—everywhere and at all times, and to have therefore a significance beyond the two cultures from which the evidences discussed are taken.

If little reference to this Essay has been made in recent decades it is perhaps due to a lack of interest among sociologists and social anthropologists in religion and therefore in its most fundamental rite. Interest in the subject appears to be reviving, and it would seem an appropriate time therefore for publication in an English translation of this remarkable piece of scholarly analysis.

I thank the Ford Foundation for assistance, through a personal grant, in the preparation of the volume.

An earlier partial translation by Arthur Julius Nelson, and without references and notes, appeared in *The Open Court*, vol. XL, 1962, pp. 33–45, 93–108, and 169–179 under the title 'The Nature and Significance of the Ceremony of Sacrifice, according to Hubert and Mauss'.

E. E. EVANS-PRITCHARD

TRANSLATOR'S NOTE

THIS STUDY OF SACRIFICE by H. Hubert and M. Mauss was first published in *L'Année sociologique*, Paris, 1898 (pp. 29–138). It was entitled 'Essai sur la Nature et la Fonction du Sacrifice'.

Certain points regarding the translation must be noted. First, the notes have been checked so far as possible, and some errors of reference corrected: but as the works cited have in some cases not been accessible, a few errors may remain. Secondly, Hebrew and Sanskrit words have been adapted to English transliteration systems, but diacritical marks have been dispensed with. Lastly, for the word 'sacrifiant', which has no exact English equivalent, the word 'sacrifier' has been coined. In the essay the 'sacrifier' is defined as 'the subject to whom the benefits of sacrifice accrue . . . or who undergoes its effect'.

W.D.H.

INTRODUCTION

OUR INTENTION IN THIS WORK is to define the
nature and social function of sacrifice. The undertaking
would be an ambitious one if the way had not been prepared for it by the researches of Tylor, Robertson Smith,
and Frazer. We are conscious of what we owe to them.
But other studies allow us to propound a theory different
from theirs, and one which seems to us more comprehensive. Moreover, we do not think of presenting it save as a
provisional hypothesis: on a subject so vast and complex,
new information in the future cannot fail to lead us to
modify our present ideas. But, with these express reser-
vations, it has seemed to us that it might be useful to co-
ordinate the facts at our disposal and to formulate an
overall conception of them.

The history of the popular and ancient concepts of the
'gift-sacrifice', the 'food-sacrifice', and the 'contract-
sacrifice', and the study of the repercussions these may
have had on ritual will not detain us, interesting as it may
be. Theories of sacrifice are as old as religions, but to find
any which have a scientific character we must look to
recent years. It is to the anthropological school, and above
all to its English representatives, that the credit for having
elaborated them must go.

Tylor,[1] inspired simultaneously by Bastian, Spencer,
and Darwin, and comparing facts borrowed from various
races and civilizations, formulated an origin for the forms

1

of sacrifice. Sacrifice, according to this writer, was originally a gift made by the primitive to supernatural beings with whom he needed to ingratiate himself. Then, when the gods grew greater and became more removed from man, the necessity of continuing to pass on this gift to them gave rise to sacrificial rites, intended to ensure that the objects thus spiritualized reached these spiritual beings. The gift was followed by homage, in which the devotee no longer expressed any hope for a return. From this it was but one step for sacrifice to become abnegation and renunciation; thus in the course of evolution the rite was carried over from the making of presents by the primitive to the sacrifice of oneself. Yet if this theory described accurately the phases of the moral development of the phenomenon, it did not account for its mechanism. On the whole, it did no more than reproduce in precise language the old, popular conceptions. Doubtless it had in itself some historical basis of truth. It is certain that usually, and to some extent, sacrifices were gifts[2] conferring on the devotee rights over his god. The gifts served also to feed the gods. But it was not sufficient to note the fact; it was necessary to account for it.

It was Robertson Smith[3] who was really the first to attempt a reasoned explanation of sacrifice. He was inspired by the recent discovery of totemism.[4] In the same way as the organization of the totemic clan had explained for him the Arab and Semitic family,[5] he saw in the practices of the totemic cult the root origin of sacrifice. In totemism the totem or the god is related to its devotees: they are of the same flesh and blood; the object of the rite is to maintain and guarantee the common life that animates them and the association that binds them together. If necessary, it re-establishes their unity. The 'blood

2

covenant' and the 'common meal' are the simplest means of obtaining this result. In the view of Robertson Smith, sacrifice is indistinguishable from these practices. According to him it was a meal at which the devotees, by eating the totem, assimilated it to themselves, were assimilated to it, and became allied with each other or with it. Sacrificial slaughter had no other object than to make possible the devouring of a sacred and consequently forbidden animal. From the communion sacrifice Robertson Smith derives the expiatory or propitiatory forms of sacrifice, namely the *piaculum* and the gift-sacrifice or honorary sacrifice. In his opinion expiation is only the reestablishment of the broken covenant; the totemic sacrifice had all the effects of an expiatory rite. Moreover, he discovers this virtue in all sacrifices, even after the complete disappearance of totemism.

It remained to be explained why the victim, originally distributed among and eaten by the devotees, was in the *piaculum* generally wholly destroyed. This was because, as soon as the ancient totems were replaced in the religion of pastoral peoples by domestic animals, they figured in sacrifices only rarely, when the circumstances were especially grave. Consequently they appeared too sacred for the profane to touch: only the priests ate of them, or rather everything was destroyed. In this case the extreme sanctity of the victim finished up by becoming impurity; the ambiguous character of sacred things, which Robertson Smith so admirably pointed out, enabled him easily to explain how such a transformation could occur. On the other hand, when the kinship between men and the animals had ceased to be understood by the Semites, human sacrifice replaced animal sacrifice, for it was henceforth the sole means of establishing a direct exchange of blood

3

between the clan and the god. But then the ideas and customs which protected the life of the individual in society by proscribing cannibalism, caused the sacrificial meal to fall into disuse.

Then again, the sacred character of domestic animals, daily profaned for the nourishment of man, gradually diminished. The divinity became separate from its animal forms. The victim, as it grew ever farther away from the god, drew nearer to man, the owner of the herd. Thus, to explain its being offered up, it came to be represented as a gift of man to the gods. In this way originated the 'gift-sacrifice'. At the same time the similarity between the rites of punishment and sacrifice, the shedding of blood which took place in both, gave a punitory character to communions of piacular origin and transformed them into expiatory sacrifices.

To these researches are linked on the one hand the studies of Frazer and on the other the theories of Jevons. More circumspect on certain points, these theories are in general the theological exaggeration of Smith's doctrine.[6] Frazer[7] adds to it an important development. Smith's explanation of the sacrifice of the god had been rudimentary. Without misunderstanding its naturalist character, he considered it as a *piaculum* of a higher order. The ancient idea of kinship between the totemic victim and the gods survived, in order to explain the annual sacrifices: they commemorated and re-enacted a drama in which the god was the victim. Frazer recognized the similarity existing between these sacrificed gods and the agrarian evil spirits of Mannhardt.[8] He compared to the totemic sacrifice the ritual murder of the spirits of vegetation. He showed how there developed, from the sacrifice and the communion meal, wherein man was reputedly assimilated to the gods, the agrarian sacrifice in which, in order to ally oneself to the god of the fields at the term of his annual life, he was killed and then eaten. Frazer established also that often the old god, when sacrificed in this way, and perhaps because of the taboos which were laid upon him, appeared to carry away with him sickness, death, and sin, and fulfilled the role of an expiatory victim and scapegoat. Yet although the idea of expulsion was prominent in these sacrifices, expiation still seemed to originate in communion. Frazer set out to supplement Smith's theory rather than to discuss it.

The great flaw in this system is that it seeks to bring the multiplicity of sacrificial forms within the unity of an arbitrarily chosen principle. First, the universality of totemism, the starting-point of the whole theory, is only a postulate. Totemism in its pure form appears only in a few isolated tribes of Australia and America. To make it the basis of all theriomorphic cults is to formulate a hypothesis which is perhaps useless, and is in any case impossible to verify. Above all, it is difficult to find sacrifices that are properly totemic. Frazer himself recognized that the totemic victim was often the victim of an agrarian sacrifice. In other cases the so-called totems are representatives of an animal species upon which depends the life of the tribe, whether it be a domesticated species, or the animal that is hunted by preference, or on the contrary one that is especially feared. At the very least a meticulous description of a certain number of these ceremonies would be required. Yet this is precisely what is lacking.

But let us accept for a moment this first hypothesis, however open to question it may be. The course of the proof is itself subject to criticism. The crux of the doctrine is the historical sequence and the logical derivation that Smith claims to establish between the communion sacrifice and other kinds of sacrifice. But nothing is more doubtful. Any attempt at a comparative chronology of the Arab, Hebrew or other sacrifices which he studied is inevitably disastrous. Those forms which appear to be most simple are known to us only through recent texts. Their simplicity itself may stem from an insufficiency of documents. In any case simplicity does not imply any priority in time. If we confine ourselves to the data of history and ethnography we find that everywhere the *piaculum* exists side by side with communion. Moreover, this vague term *piaculum* allows Smith to describe, under the same heading and in the same terms, purifications, propitiations, and expiations, and it is this confusion that prevents him from analysing the expiatory sacrifice. Undoubtedly these sacrifices are usually followed by a reconciliation with the god; a sacrificial meal, a sprinkling of blood, or an anointing re-establish the covenant. Only, for Smith, it is in these communion rites themselves that the purifying force of these kinds of sacrifices resides; the idea of expiation is thus engulfed in the idea of communion. Undoubtedly he discovers in some extreme or simplified forms something that he does not venture to link with communion, a kind of exorcism, the driving out of an evil spirit. But in his opinion these are magical processes which involve no element of sacrifice, and he explains with much learning and ingenuity their tardy introduction into the mechanism of sacrifice. But this is precisely what we cannot grant. One of the aims of this work is to demonstrate that the expulsion of a sacred spirit, whether pure or impure, is a primordial component of sacrifice, as primordial and irreducible as communion.

If the system of sacrifice has any unity, it must be sought elsewhere.

Robertson Smith's error was above all one of method. Instead of analysing in its original complexity the Semitic ritual system, he set about classifying the facts genealogically, in accordance with the analogical connexions that he believed he saw between them. This is a characteristic common to English anthropologists, who are concerned above all with collecting and classifying documents. For our part, we do not desire to build up in our turn an encyclopedic survey which we could not make complete and which, coming after theirs, would serve no purpose. We shall try to study thoroughly typical facts, which we shall glean particularly from Sanskrit texts and from the Bible. We are far from having documents of equal value concerning Greek and Roman sacrifices. By comparing scattered pieces of information provided by inscriptions and writers, only an ill-assorted ritual can be built up. On the other hand, we have in the Bible and in the Hindu texts collections of doctrines that belong to a definite era. The document is direct, drawn up by the participants themselves in their own language, in the very spirit in which they enacted the rites, even if not always with a very clear consciousness of the origin and motive of their actions.

Doubtless, when we are seeking to disentangle the simple and elementary forms of an institution, it is disconcerting to take as our starting-point for the investigation complicated rituals of recent date that have been commented upon and probably distorted by theological scholarship. But in this category of facts all purely historical investigations are fruitless. The antiquity of the texts or of the facts recounted, the comparative barbarity of the peoples and the apparent simplicity of the rites are deceptive chronological indications. It is too much to seek in an anthology of lines from the *Iliad* even a rough picture of primitive Greek sacrifice; they do not even suffice to give us an exact idea of sacrifice in Homeric times. We only glimpse the most ancient rites through literary documents that are vague and incomplete, fragmentary and misleading remnants, traditions lacking in fidelity. It is likewise impossible to hope to glean from ethnography alone the pattern of primitive institutions. Generally distorted through over-hasty observation or falsified by the exactness of our languages, the facts recorded by ethnographers have value only if they are compared with more precise and more complete documents.

We do not therefore propose here to trace the history and genesis of sacrifice, and if we speak of priority, we mean it in a logical and not an historical sense. Not that we forgo the right to refer to classical texts or to ethnology in order to throw light upon our analysis and to check the general character of our conclusions. But, instead of directing our studies to artificially constituted groupings of facts, in the well-defined and complete rituals that we shall treat we shall have entities already determined and natural systems of rites that command attention. Restricted in this way by the texts, we shall be less liable to omission or arbitrary classification. Lastly, because the two religions that are to form the centre of our investigations are very different, since one leads to monotheism and the other to pantheism, we may hope by comparing them to arrive at conclusions that are sufficiently general.[9]

Chapter One

DEFINITION AND UNITY OF THE SACRIFICIAL SYSTEM

IT IS IMPORTANT, before proceeding further, to give an overall definition of the facts that we designate under the heading of sacrifice.

The word 'sacrifice' immediately suggests the idea of consecration, and one might be tempted to believe that the two notions are identical. It is indeed certain that sacrifice always implies a consecration; in every sacrifice an object passes from the common into the religious domain; it is consecrated. But not all consecrations are of the same kind. In some the effects are limited to the consecrated object, be it a man or a thing. This is, for example, the case with unction. When a king is consecrated, his religious personality alone is modified; apart from this, nothing is changed. In sacrifice, on the other hand, the consecration extends beyond the thing consecrated; among other objects, it touches the moral person who bears the expenses of the ceremony. The devotee who provides the victim which is the object of the consecration is not, at the completion of the operation, the same as he was at the beginning. He has acquired a religious character which he did not have before, or has rid himself of an unfavourable character with which he was affected;

he has raised himself to a state of grace or has emerged from a state of sin. In either case he has been religiously transformed.

We give the name 'sacrifier' to the subject to whom the benefits of sacrifice thus accrue, or who undergoes its effects.[10] This subject is sometimes an individual,[11] sometimes a collectivity[12]—a family, a clan, a tribe, a nation, a secret society. When it is a collectivity it may be that the group fulfils collectively the function of the sacrifier, that is, it attends the sacrifice as a body;[13] but sometimes it delegates one of its members who acts in its stead and place. Thus the family is generally represented by its head,[14] society by its magistrates.[15] This is a first step in that succession of representations which we shall encounter at every one of the stages of sacrifice.

There are, however, cases where the effects of the sacrificial consecration are exerted not directly on the sacrifier himself, but on certain things which appertain more or less directly to his person. In the sacrifice that takes place at the building of a house,[16] it is the house that is affected by it, and the quality that it acquires by this means can survive longer than its owner for the time being. In other cases, it is the sacrifier's field, the river he has to cross, the oath he takes, the treaty he makes, etc. We shall call those kinds of things for whose sake the sacrifice takes place *objects of sacrifice*. It is important, moreover, to notice that the sacrifier himself is also affected through his presence at the sacrifice and through the interest or part he takes in it. The ambit of action of the sacrifice is especially noteworthy here, for it produces a double effect, one on the object for which it is offered and upon which it is desired to act, the other on the moral person who desires and instigates that effect. Sometimes even it is only of use provided it brings about this twofold result. When the father of a family offers a sacrifice for the inauguration of his house, not only must the house be capable of receiving his family, but they must be fit to enter it.[17]

We see what is the distinctive characteristic of consecration in sacrifice: the thing consecrated serves as an intermediary between the sacrifier, or the object which is to receive the practical benefits of the sacrifice, and the divinity to whom the sacrifice is usually addressed. Man and the god are not in direct contact. In this way sacrifice is distinguished from most of the facts grouped under the heading of blood covenant in which by the exchange of blood a direct fusion of human and divine life is brought about.[18] The same will be said about certain instances of the offering of hair. Here again, the subject who sacrifices is in direct communication with the god through the part of his person which is offered up.[19] Doubtless there are connexions between these rites and sacrifice; but they must be distinguished from it.

But this first characteristic is not enough, for it does not allow us to distinguish sacrifice from those acts, inadequately defined, which may fittingly be termed offerings. There is indeed no offering in which the object consecrated is not likewise interposed between the god and the offerer, and in which the latter is not affected by the consecration. But if every sacrifice is in effect an oblation, there are oblations of different kinds. Sometimes the object consecrated is simply presented as a votive offering; consecration can assign it to the service of the god, but it does not change its nature by the mere fact that it is made to pass into the religious domain. Those oblations of the firstfruits which were merely brought to the temple, remained there untouched and belonged to the priests. On the other hand, in other cases consecration destroys the object offered up; if an animal is offered on the altar, the desired end is reached only when its throat has been cut, or it is cut to pieces or consumed by fire, in short, *sacrificed*. The object thus destroyed is the *victim*. It is clearly for oblations of this kind that the name sacrifice must be reserved. We may surmise that the difference between these two kinds of operation depends upon their different degrees of solemnity and their differing efficacy. In the case of sacrifice, the religious energy released is stronger. From this arises the havoc it causes.

In these conditions we must designate as sacrifice any oblation, even of vegetable matter, whenever the offering or part of it is destroyed, although usage seems to limit the word sacrifice to designate only sacrifices where blood is shed. To restrict the meaning of the name in this way is arbitrary. Due allowance having been made, the mechanism of consecration is the same in all cases; there is consequently no objective reason for distinguishing between them. Thus the Hebrew *minha* is an oblation of flour and cakes[10] which accompanies certain sacrifices. Yet it is so much a sacrifice like these other sacrifices that Leviticus does not distinguish between them.[11] The same rites are observed. A portion is destroyed on the altar fire, the remainder being eaten entirely or in part by the priests. In Greece[12] only vegetable oblations were permitted on the altar of certain gods;[13] thus there were sacrificial rites which did not involve animal oblations. The same may be said of libations of milk, wine, or other liquids.[14] They are subject in Greece[15] to the same distinctions as sacrifices;[16] on occasion they can even replace them.[17] The identity of these different operations was so clearly felt by the Hindus that the objects offered up in these different cases were themselves considered identical. They are all considered as equally living, and are treated as such. Thus in a sacrifice considered to be of sufficient solemnity, when the grains are crushed they are implored not to avenge themselves upon the sacrifier for the hurt done them. When the cakes are placed upon the potsherds to bake, they are requested not to break;[18] when they are cut, they are entreated not to injure the sacrifier and the priests. When a libation of milk is made —and all Hindu libations are made with milk or a milk product—it is not something inanimate that is offered up, but the cow itself, in its liquid essence, its sap, its fertility.[19]

Thus we finally arrive at the following definition: *Sacrifice is a religious act which, through the consecration of a victim, modifies the condition of the moral person who accomplishes it or that of certain objects with which he is concerned.*[20]

For brevity of exposition we shall call those sacrifices in which the personality of the sacrifier is directly affected by the sacrifice *personal sacrifices*, and those in which objects, real or ideal, receive directly the sacrificial action *objective sacrifices*.

This definition not only restricts the object of our investigations, but also settles for us a very important point: it presupposes the generic unity of sacrifices. Thus as we allowed ourselves to surmise when we reproached Smith with reducing the expiatory sacrifice to a communion sacrifice, it was not to establish the original and irreducible diversity of sacrificial systems. It was because their unity, though real, was not of the kind he claimed.

But this first result appears to contradict the endless variety which at first sight the forms of sacrifice seem to present. The occasions of sacrifice are innumerable, the effects desired are very diverse, and the multiplicity of ends implies that of means. Thus the custom has been adopted, above all in Germany, of classifying sacrifices in a certain number of distinct categories: for example, one speaks of expiatory sacrifices (*Sühnopfer*), of sacrifices of thanksgiving (*Dankopfer*), of sacrifices of request (*Bittopfer*), etc. But in reality the demarcations between these categories are vague, confused, and often indiscernible; the same practices are to be found to some extent in all of them. We shall not adopt any of the classifications usually employed; they do not, in our opinion, result from a methodical investigation. Without attempting to propound a new classification which would be open to the same objections, in order to have an idea of the diversity of sacrifices we shall content ourselves here with borrowing one of the classifications given in Hindu texts.

Perhaps the most instructive is that which divides sacrifices into regular and occasional.[31] Occasional sacrifices are, firstly, sacramental sacrifices (*samskara*), namely those which accompany the solemn moments of life. A certain number of these are part of the domestic ritual (as laid down in the *Grihya sutras*): those that take place at birth, at the rite of tonsure, on the departure of a ward, at marriage, etc. Others are part of the solemn ritual; such are the anointing of a king, and the sacrifice conferring religious and civil attributes which are considered superior to all others.[32] Secondly, there are votive sacrifices whose occasional nature is even more marked;[33] lastly, there are curative and expiatory sacrifices. As for the regular or, better, periodical sacrifices (*nityani*), they

14

are linked to certain fixed moments of time, independent of men's will and of chance circumstance. Such are the daily sacrifice, the sacrifice at new and full moon, the sacrifices at seasonal and pastoral festivals, and the first-fruits at the year's end. All are generally found both in the solemn and the domestic ritual, with differences appropriate to the solemnity of the one and the family character of the other.

We see for how many different occasions the Brahmins made sacrifices serve. But at the same time they felt so deeply the unity of them all that they made this the basis of their theory. Almost all the texts of the solemn ritual follow the same plan: the exposition of a basic rite that is gradually diversified to make it correspond to different needs.[14] Thus the *shrauta sutras* and the *brahmanas* which comment upon them start from a general description of the whole of the rites that constitute the sacrifice of cakes at the new and full moon, and it is this scheme which is successively adapted, modified according to circumstances, to all the ceremonies in which the cake sacrifice figures. Thus a cake sacrifice constitutes the essential ceremony both for seasonal festivals, whose aspects are already so numerous and varied (sacrifices to nature, sacrifices of purification, of the consumption of the first seeds, etc.), as well as for a whole series of votive sacrifices.[15] And this is not a mere device of exposition, but there is in it a real sense of the flexibility of the sacrificial system. Let us take the solemn animal sacrifice. We find it existing separately or combined with others, in the most varied cases—in the periodical festivals of nature and of vegetation, and in the occasional rites such as the building of an altar, or in rites whose object is to redeem the individual. As for the sacrifice of the *soma*,[16] since soma is suited for sacrifice only in spring, this can only be a periodical festival.[37] Yet soma is sacrificed for a multiplicity of ends which sometimes depend upon and sometimes are independent of vows and occasions: at every spring, at the consecration of the king, to reach a higher rank in society, to become invulnerable and victorious, to escape from misfortunes that threaten to become permanent. In the same way rites of the opposite kind may have the same intention: internal reasons must have been the cause for which the sterile cow sacrificed by the Brahmins to Rudra, the evil god, is sacrificed in the same manner as the goat to the beneficent heavenly gods Agni and Soma.[38]

The Hebrew ritual provides no less striking examples of the complexity of the rites and the identical nature of their component elements. Leviticus reduces all sacrifices to four basic forms: *'olah, hattat, shelamim, minha.*[39] The names of two of these are significant. The *hattat* was the sacrifice employed especially to expiate the sin called *hattat* or *hataah*, the definition of which given in Leviticus is unfortunately extremely vague.[40] The *shelamim*[41] (LXX θυσία εἰρηνική) is a communion sacrifice, a sacrifice of thanksgiving, of alliance, of vows. As for the terms *'olah* and *minha*, they are purely descriptive. Each recalls one of the special operations of the sacrifice: the latter, the presentation of the victim, if it is of vegetable matter; the former, the dispatch of the offering to the divinity.[42]

This simplification of the system of sacrifices[43] is doubtless the result of a classification too specialized, and moreover, too arbitrary, to serve as a basis for a general study of sacrifice. But in reality these four typical forms are not, or at least are no longer, real types of sacrifice, but kinds of abstract component elements in which one of the organs of sacrifice is particularly developed; these elements can always enter into more complex formulas. The ritual split up the ceremonies to which each occasion to sacrifice gave rise into a multiplicity of sacrifices that were simple or were considered so. For instance, the sacrifice at the ordination of the high priest[44] is made up of a *hattat*, the expiatory sacrifice; of an *'olah*, the sacrifice in which the victim is wholly burnt; and of the sacrifice of the ram of consecrations, which is a *zebah shelamim*, a communion sacrifice. The sacrifice for the purification of women after childbirth includes a *hattat* and an *'olah*.[45] The sacrifice for the cleansing of a leper includes rites analogous to those for the consecration of the priest.[46] Thus there are here two sacrifices, one apparently expiatory and the other of communion, which end up by being similar rites. Thus even these two irreducible ideas of expiation and of communion, of communication of a sacred quality and of expulsion of an opposing quality, cannot form the basis for a general and rigorous classification of sacrifices. We would perhaps seek in vain for examples of an expiatory sacrifice into which no element of communion is interpolated, or for examples of communion sacrifices which do not in some respect resemble expiatory ones.[47]

For we discover the same ambiguity not only in complex sacrifices, but even in the elementary sacrifices of the Pentateuch. The *zebah shelamim*[48] is a communion sacrifice. Yet certain parts of the victim—the blood, the fat, or some of the entrails—are always placed on one side, destroyed, or become prohibited. One limb is always eaten by the priests. The victim of the *hattat* may be assigned entirely to the priests;[49] failing the sacrifier, the sacrificers communicate. In the *hattat* celebrated for the

17

consecration or purification of the temple or the altar, the blood of the victim is used to anoint the doors and walls. This rite endows them with consecration.[60] Now a rite of the same nature is to be found in the *zebah shelamim* of ordination; an exactly similar anointing with blood is performed upon Aaron and his sons.[61]

These examples show the affinity that links practices which in their aim and results seem completely opposed. There is a continuity between the forms of sacrifice. They are both too diverse and yet too similar for it to be possible to divide them into over-specialized categories. They are all the same in essence, and it is this which constitutes their unity. They are the outer coverings of one single mechanism that we now propose to dismantle and describe.

Chapter Two

THE SCHEME OF SACRIFICE

The Entry

IT IS EVIDENT that we cannot hope here to sketch out an abstract scheme of sacrifice comprehensive enough to suit all known cases; the variety of facts is too great. All that can be done is to study specific forms of sacrifice that are complex enough for all the important moments of the drama to be included in them and well enough known for an exact analysis to be made. The sacrifice which seems to us to answer best to these conditions is the Vedic Hindu sacrifice of animals. Indeed we know of no other in which the details are better explained. All the participants are very clearly presented at the time of their entrance and exit as well as during the course of the action. Moreover, it is an amorphous rite; it is not orientated in a fixed direction, but may serve the most diverse ends. There is thus no sacrifice that lends itself better to the investigation we desire to undertake. For this reason we shall make it the foundation of our study, except for grouping around the analysis of it other facts taken either from India iteslf or from other religions.

Sacrifice is a religious act that can only be carried out in a religious atmosphere and by means of essentially religious agents. But, in general, before the ceremony neither sacrifier nor sacrificer, nor place, instruments, or victim, possess this characteristic to a suitable degree. The first phase of the sacrifice is intended to impart it to them. They are profane; their condition must be changed. To do this, rites are necessary to introduce them into the sacred world and involve them in it, more or less profoundly, according to the importance of the part they have subsequently to play. It is this which constitutes, in the very words of the Sanskrit texts,[52] *the entry into the sacrifice.*

(1) *The sacrifier.* In order to study the manner in which this change in condition is effected in the sacrifier, let us at once take an extreme, almost abnormal case, which does not belong to the ritual of animal sacrifice, but in which the common rites are as it were enlarged, and consequently more easily observable. The case is that of the *diksha*, namely, the preparation of the sacrifier for the sacrifice of the soma.[53] As soon as the priests have been selected, a whole series of symbolic ceremonies begins for the sacrifier. These will progressively strip him of the temporal being that he possessed, in order to cause him to be reborn in an entirely new form. All that touches upon the gods must be divine; the sacrifier is obliged to become a god himself in order to be capable of acting upon them.[54] To this end a special hut is built for him, tightly enclosed, for the dikshita is a god and the world of the gods is separated from that of men.[55] He is shaved and his nails are cut,[56] but according to the fashion of the gods—that is to say, in the opposite order to that which is usually followed among men.[57] After taking a bath of purification,[58] he dons a brand-new linen garment,[59] thereby indicating that a new existence is about to begin for him. Then, after various anointings,[60] he is dressed in the skin of a black antelope.[61] This is the solemn moment when

the new creature stirs within him. He has become a foetus. His head is veiled and he is made to clench his fists,⁶² for the embryo in its bag has its fists clenched. He is made to walk around the hearth just as the foetus moves within the womb. He remains in this state until the great ceremony of the introduction of the soma.⁶³ Then he unclenches his fists, he unveils himself, he is born into the divine existence, he is a god.

But once his divine nature has been proclaimed,⁶⁴ it confers upon him the rights and imposes upon him the duties of a god, or at least those of a holy man. He must have no contact with men of impure caste, nor with women; he does not reply to those who question him; he must not be touched.⁶⁵ Being a god, he is dispensed from all sacrifice. He consumes only milk, the food of fasting. And this existence lasts for many long months until his body has become translucent. Then, having as it were sacrificed his former body⁶⁶ and attained the highest degree of nervous excitement, he is fit to sacrifice, and the ceremonies begin.

This complicated, long-drawn-out initiation required for ceremonies of exceptional gravity is only, it is true, an amplification. But it is found, although in a less developed degree, in the preparatory rites for ordinary animal sacrifice. In this case it is no longer necessary for the sacrifier to become divine, but he must still become sacred. For this reason here also he shaves himself, bathes, abstains from all sexual relationships, fasts and keeps vigil, etc.⁶⁷ And even for these more simple rites the interpretations that are given to them by the accompanying prayers and the Brahmanic commentaries clearly indicate their purport. We read at the very beginning of the *Shatapatha Brahmana*, '[The sacrifier] rinses his mouth. . . . For before this he is unfit for sacrifice. . . . For the waters are pure. He becomes pure within. . . . *He passes from the world of men into the world of the gods.*'[68]

These rites are not peculiar to the Hindus: the Semitic world, Greece, and Rome also provide examples of them. A certain degree of relationship with the god is demanded first of all from those who wish to be admitted to the sacrifice.[69] Thus the stranger is generally excluded from it,[70] and even more so courtesans, slaves,[71] and often women.[72] Moreover, temporary purity is required.[73] The advent of the divinity is terrible for those that are impure;[74] when Yahweh was about to appear on Sinai, the people had to wash their garments and remain chaste.[75] In the same way the sacrifice is preceded by a more or less lengthy period of purification.[76] This consists principally of sprinklings with lustral water and ablutions.[77] Sometimes the sacrifier must fast[78] and purge himself.[79] He must put on clean garments,[80] or even special ones[81] which impart to him a first touch of sanctity. Roman ritual also generally prescribed the wearing of the veil, the sign of separation and consequently of consecration.[82] The crown that the sacrifier wore on his head, whilst warding off evil spirits, marked him as having a sacred character.[83] Sometimes the sacrifier completed his physical preparations by shaving his head and eyebrows.[84] All these purifications,[85] lustrations, and consecrations prepared the profane participant for the sacred act, by eliminating from his body the imperfections of his secular nature, cutting him off from the common life, and introducing him step by step into the sacred world of the gods.

(2) *The sacrificer.* There are sacrifices in which there are no other participants than the sacrifier and the victim. But generally one does not venture to approach sacred

things directly and alone; they are too lofty and serious a matter. An intermediary, or at the very least a guide, is necessary.[44] This is the priest. More familiar with the world of the gods, in which he is partly involved through a previous consecration,[47] he can approach it more closely and with less fear than the layman, who is perhaps sullied by unknown blemishes. At the same time he prevents the sacrifier from committing fatal errors. Sometimes the profane person is even formally excluded from the sanctuary and the sacrifice.[48] In this case the priest becomes, on the one hand, the mandatory of the sacrifier,[49] whose condition he shares and whose sins he bears.[50] On the other hand, however, he is sealed with a divine seal.[51] He bears the name,[52] the title,[53] or the robe[54] of his god. He is his minister, even his incarnate presence,[55] or at the very least the repository of his power. He is the visible agent of consecration in the sacrifice. In short, he stands on the threshold of the sacred and the profane world and represents them both at one and the same time. They are linked in him.

Because of his religious character, it might be supposed that he at least can enter upon the sacrifice without any preliminary initiation. This is in fact what took place in India. The Brahmin appeared with a nature almost entirely divine. Thus he had no need for a special consecration, save in extraordinary circumstances[56]—for there are rites that require a previous preparation by the sacrificer as well as by the sacrifier. This differs from that which we have described for the layman only inasmuch as it is generally less complex. As the priest is naturally nearer to the sacred world, simpler operations are enough to enable him to enter it completely.

Among the Hebrews, despite the fact that the priest

was ordained, he had to take certain extra precautions in order to be able to sacrifice. He had to wash before entering the sanctuary.[97] Before the ceremony he had to abstain from wine and fermented liquids.[98] He put on linen garments,[99] which he took off immediately after the sacrifice.[100] He laid these away in a consecrated place, for they had already become holy, fearful objects which were dangerous for the profane to touch.[101] In his intercourse with the divine—although this was habitual for him—the priest himself was perpetually under the threat of the supernatural death[102] that had struck down Aaron's two sons,[103] and those of Eli,[104] as well as the priests of the family of Baithos.[105] By increasing his personal sanctity,[106] he made the difficult approach to the sanctuary easier, and safeguarded himself.

But he did not sanctify himself wholly for his own sake: he did so also on behalf of the person or society in whose name he was acting. Because he exposed to danger not only himself but those whose delegate he was, he was obliged to take even greater precautions. This was particularly noticeable at the festival of the Great Pardon.[107] Indeed, on that day the high priest represents the people of Israel. He seeks pardon for himself and for Israel—for himself and his family by the bullock, for Israel by the two goats.[108] Only after this expiation, and having set light to the incense, does he penetrate behind the veil of the Holy of Holies,[109] where he finds God in the cloud. Such grave functions required very special preparations, as befitted the quasi-divine role that the priest fulfilled. Due allowance being made, the rites resemble those of the *diksha* discussed above. Seven days before the feast the high priest shuts himself off from his family,[110] and remains in the cell of the *paredri* (the assessors).[111] Like the Hindu sacrifier, he is the object of all sorts of attentions. The evening before, old men sit round and read to him the section of the Bible in which is laid down the ritual of Kippur. He is given little to eat. Then he is conducted into a special room,[112] where he is left alone after having been adjured to change nothing in the rites. 'Then, both he and they weeping, they parted.'[113] The whole night long he must stay awake,[114] for sleep is a time during which defilements may unwittingly be contracted.[115] Thus the entire pontifical rite tends toward the same purpose: to give the high priest an exceptional sanctity[116] which will enable him to draw near to the god hidden behind the mercy-seat and to bear the burden of the sins that will be heaped upon his head.

(3) *The place, the instruments.* For the sacrifice proper to begin, it is not enough for the sacrifier and the priest to be sanctified. It cannot take place at any time or anywhere. For not all times of the day or year are equally propitious for sacrifice; there are even times at which it must be ruled out. In Assyria, for example, it was forbidden on the 7th, 14th, and 21st of the month.[117] According to the nature and the purpose of the ceremony, the hour of celebration differed. Sometimes it had to be offered during the daytime;[118] sometimes, on the other hand, during the evening or at night.[119]

The place of the ceremony must itself be sacred: outside a holy place immolation is mere murder.[120] When the sacrifice is performed in a temple[121] or in a place already sacred in itself, preliminary consecration is unnecessary or at least is very much shortened. This is the case with the Hebrew sacrifice as laid down in the ritual of the Pentateuch. It was celebrated in a single sanctuary consecrated beforehand,[122] chosen by the divinity[123] and made divine by his presence.[124] Thus the texts that have come down to us contain no provisions relating to the repeated sanctifying of the place of sacrifice. Nevertheless, the purity and sanctity of the temple and the sanctuary had to be maintained: daily sacrifices[125] and an annual ceremony of expiation were the means of fulfilling this need.[126] The Hindus had no temple. Each could choose for himself the place where he wished to sacrifice.[127] But this place had to be consecrated in advance by means of a certain number of rites, of which the most essential was the setting up of the fires.[128] We shall not describe it in detail. The complicated ceremonies of which it is made up have as their object the kindling of a fire in which only pure elements, already consecrated to Agni,[129] will enter. One of these fires is even kindled by friction, so that it is entirely new.[130] In these conditions there is a magical power which wards off evil spirits, harmful spells, and devils. The fire is the slayer of demons.[131] It is even more than this: it is the god, it is Agni in his complete form.[132] In the same way, according to certain Biblical legends also, the fire of sacrifice is none other than the divinity itself, which consumes the victim, or, to put it more exactly, the fire is the sign of consecration which sets it on fire.[133] What is divine in the fire of the Hindu sacrifice is thus transmitted to the place of sacrifice and consecrates it.[134] This site consisted of a fairly large rectangular space, called the *vihara*.[135]

Within this area is another space called the *vedi*, whose sacred character is even more pronounced. This corresponds to the altar. Thus the *vedi* occupies a position even more central than the fires. These, indeed, contrary to what is the case in most other cults, are not on the altar itself, but surround it.[136] The outline of the *vedi* is carefully marked out on the ground;[137] to do this a spade is taken—or in other cases, the magical wooden sword—and the earth is lightly touched with it, with the words 'The wicked one is killed.'[138] By this all impurity is destroyed; the magic circle is traced out, the site is consecrated. Within the boundaries thus delimited, the ground is dug and levelled; the hole formed in this way constitutes the altar. After a lustration that is both expiatory and purificatory the bottom of the hole is covered with different kinds of turf. It is on this turf that the gods to whom the sacrifice is addressed come and sit; there, invisible yet present, they attend the ceremony.[139]

We shall not describe in detail the various instruments[140] which are laid upon the altar,[141] after having been either made *ad hoc* or carefully purified. But one of them must claim our attention, for it really forms part of the altar.[142] This is the *yupa*, the stake to which the animal is to be bound. It is not a piece of rough wood, but the tree from which it was hewn had already in itself a divine nature,[143] which unctions and libations have further reinforced.[144] It also occupies a prominent position, for it is there that the victim will stand, the most important of all the visible personages that will take part in the ceremony.[145] Therefore the Brahmanas represent it as one of the points at which all the religious forces that are in operation in the sacrifice converge and are concentrated. By its slender trunk, it recalls the manner in which the gods mounted up to heaven;[146] by its upper section it gives power over heavenly things, by its middle part, over the things of the air, by its lower part, over those of the earth.[147] But at the same time it represents the sacrifier. It is the height of the sacrifier that determines its dimensions.[148] When it is anointed, the sacrifier is anointed; when it is made firm, it is the sacrifier that is strengthened.[149] In it takes place, in a more marked manner than in the priest, that communication, that fusion of the gods and the sacrifier, which will become even more marked in the victim.[150]

The scene is now set. The actors are ready. The entry of the victim will mark the beginning of the drama. But before introducing it, we must point out an essential characteristic of the sacrifice: the perfect continuity that is necessary to it. From the moment that it has begun,[151] it must continue to the end without interruption and in the ritual order. All the operations of which it is composed must follow each other in turn without a break. The forces at work, if they are not directed in exactly the way prescribed, elude both sacrifier and priest and turn upon them in a terrible fashion.[152] Even this outward continuity of the rites is not enough.[153] There must also be a like constancy in the mental state of sacrifier and sacrificer, concerning the gods, the victim, and the prayer that one wants answered.[154] They must have unshakeable confidence in the automatic result of the sacrifice. In short, a religious act must be accomplished in a religious frame of mind: the inward attitude must correspond to the external one.[155] We see how, from the very outset, sacrifice demanded a *credo* (*shraddha* is the equivalent of *credo*, even philologically), and how the act carried faith with it.[156]

THE VICTIM

We said above that in the Hindu rite the construction of the altar consists in describing a magic circle on the ground. In reality all the operations we have just considered have the same purpose. They consist in tracing out a kind of series of concentric magic circles within the sacred area. In the outer circle stands the sacrifier; then come in turn the priest, the altar, and the stake. On the perimeter, where stands the layman on whose behalf the sacrifice takes place, the religious atmosphere is weak and minimal. It increases as the space in which it is developed grows smaller. The whole activity of the place of sacrifice is thus organized and concentrated round a single focus. Everything converges on the victim who is now about to appear. Everything is ready for its reception. It is brought in.

Sometimes it was consecrated by the mere fact of its birth: the species to which it belonged was joined to the divinity by special links.[157] Having thus a divine character by nature, it did not need to acquire one specially for the occasion. But, more usually, fixed rites were necessary to confer upon it the religious condition that its destined role demanded. In certain cases where it had been marked out long before, these ceremonies had taken place before it was brought to the place of sacrifice.[158] But often at that moment it still had nothing sacred about it. It was merely in a state to fulfil certain conditions that made it eligible to receive consecration. It had to be without defect, sickness, or infirmity.[159] It had to be of a certain colour,[160] age, and sex, according to the result to be brought about.[161] But to bring this general aptitude into action, to raise it to the required level of religiosity, the victim had to submit to a whole gamut of ceremonies.

In certain countries it was dressed up,[162] painted or whitened, like the *bos cretatus* of Roman sacrifices. Its horns were gilded,[163] a crown was placed upon it, it was bedecked with ribbons.[164] These adornments imparted to it a religious character. Sometimes even the costume that was put on it brought it closer to the god who presided over the sacrifice: this was the purpose of the disguises used in the agrarian sacrifices, of which traces only remain.[165] The semi-consecration thus conferred upon it could moreover be obtained in another way. In Mexico[166] and at Rhodes[167] the victim was made drunk. This drunkenness was a sign of possession. The divine spirit was already pervading the victim.

But the Hindu ritual will enable us to follow more closely the whole series of operations in the course of which the victim is progressively made divine. After it has been bathed,[168] it is brought in, whilst various libations are made.[169] It is then addressed, laudatory epithets being heaped upon it, and it is exhorted to keep calm.[170] At the same time the god who is the lord of the animals is invoked, in order to ask him to agree to the use of his property as a victim.[171] These precautions, propitiations, and marks of honour serve a dual purpose. Firstly, they acknowledge the sacred character of the victim: by being termed something excellent, the property of the gods, it becomes so. But above all it must be persuaded to allow itself to be sacrificed peaceably, for the welfare of men, and not to take vengeance once it is dead. These usages, which are extremely frequent,[172] do not signify, as has been said, that the beast sacrificed is always a former totemic animal. The explanation lies closer at hand. There is in the victim a spirit which it is the very aim of the sacrifice to liberate. This spirit must therefore be conciliated, for otherwise it might become dangerous when freed; hence the flattery and preliminary apologies.

Then the victim is bound to the stake. At that moment the sacred character it is in the act of acquiring is already so great that the Brahmin can no longer touch it with his hands, and the sacrifier himself hesitates to approach it. He must be invited to do so, and encouraged by a special formula addressed to him by a priest.[173] Yet, in order to develop this religiosity, already so intense, to the utmost extent, three series of rites are required. The animal is given water to drink,[174] for water is divine; its body is lustrated above, beneath, and on every part.[175] Then it is anointed with melted butter on the head, then on the withers, the shoulders, the croup, and between the horns. These anointings correspond to those which were made with oil in Hebrew sacrifice, to the ceremony of the *mola salsa* in Rome, or to the οὐλαί or barley grains that in Greece the bystanders threw upon the animal.[176] Likewise, almost everywhere are to be found libations analogous to those of which we have just spoken. They had as their purpose to heap sanctity on the victim. Lastly, after these lustrations and anointings there comes in the Vedic ritual a final ceremony whose effect is to enclose the victim itself in a final magic circle, smaller and more divine than the others. From the fire of the gods a priest plucks a brand, and with it in his hand walks three times round the animal. This circumambulation took place in India round all the victims, with or without fire. It was the god Agni who surrounded the animal on all sides, consecrated it, and set it apart.[177]

Yet, even while continuing to move onward into the world of the gods, the victim had to remain in touch with mankind. In the religions we are considering here, the means used to ensure this contact are provided by the principles of magical and religious sympathy. Sometimes there is a direct and natural representation: a father is represented by his son, whom he sacrifices, etc.[178] In general, since a sacrifier is always obliged to undertake the expenses in person, there is, by virtue of this very fact, a more or less complete representation.[179] But in other cases this association of the victim and the sacrifier is brought about by a physical contact between the sacrifier (sometimes the priest) and the victim. This contact is obtained, in Semitic ritual, by the laying on of hands, and in others by equivalent rites.[180] Through this proximity the victim, who already represents the gods, comes to represent the sacrifier also. Indeed, it is not enough to say that it represents him: it is merged in him. The two personalities are fused together. At least in the Hindu ritual this identification even becomes so complete that from then onwards the future fate of the victim, its imminent death, has a kind of reverse effect upon the sacrifier. Hence an ambiguous situation results for the latter. He needs to touch the animal in order to remain united with it, and yet is afraid to do so, for in so doing he runs the risk of sharing its fate. The ritual resolves the difficulty by taking a middle course. The sacrifier touches the victim only through the priest, who himself only touches it through the intermediary of one of the instruments of sacrifice.[181] Thus this process of drawing together the sacred and the profane, which we have seen come about progressively through the various elements of the sacrifice, is completed in the victim.

We have now arrived at the culminating point of the ceremony. All the elements of the sacrifice are now present; they have been brought into contact for the last time. But the supreme act remains to be accomplished.[182] The victim is already sanctified to an extreme degree. But the spirit residing in it, the divine principle which it now contains, is still pent up in its body and attached by this last link to the world of profane things. Death will release it, thereby making the consecration definitive and irrevocable. This is the solemn moment.

That which now begins is a crime, a kind of sacrilege. So, while the victim was being led to the place of slaughter, some rituals prescribed libations and expiations.[163] Excuses were made for the act that was about to be carried out, the death of the animal was lamented,[164] one wept for it as one would weep for a relative. Its pardon was asked before it was struck down. The rest of the species to which it belonged were harangued, as if they were one vast family, entreated not to avenge the wrong about to be done them in the person of one of their number.[165] Under the influence of these same ideas[166] the instigator of the slaughter might be punished by beating[167] or exile. At Athens the priest at the sacrifice of the *Bouphonia* fled, casting his axe away. All those who had taken part in the sacrifice were called to the Prytaneion. They threw the blame upon each other. Finally, the knife was condemned and thrown into the sea.[168] The purifications which the sacrificer had to undergo after the sacrifice resembled moreover the expiation of a criminal.[169]

So, once the beast is placed in the prescribed position and turned in the direction laid down in the rites,[170] everyone keeps silence. In India the priests turn round. The sacrifier and the officiating priest also turn round,[171] murmuring propitiatory mantras.[172] Nothing is to be heard save the orders given in a simple voice by the priest to the sacrifier. The latter then tightens the bond that encircles the neck of the animal,[173] and 'quietens its breath',[174] as the euphemism employed has it. The victim is dead; the spirit has departed.

The rites of slaughter were extremely variable. But every cult insisted that they be scrupulously observed. To modify them was generally a fatal heresy, punishable by excommunication and death.[195] This was because the act of slaughter released an ambiguous force—or rather a blind one, terrible by the very fact that it was a force. It therefore had to be limited, directed, and tamed; this was what the rites were for. Most usually the nape of the victim's neck, or the neck itself, was severed.[196] Stoning was an ancient rite that no longer took place in Judaea except in certain cases of penal execution, or in Greece except as a token in the ritual of some festivals.[197] Elsewhere the victim was knocked senseless[198] or hanged,[199] So serious an operation could not be accompanied by too many precautions. For the most part it was wished that death should be prompt, and the passage of the victim from its earthly life to its divine one was hastened so as not to leave evil influences time to vitiate the sacrificial act. If the animal's cries were held to be bad omens, an attempt was made to stifle or prevent them.[200] Often, in order to avoid any possible deviations once consecration had taken place, the attempt was made to control the effusion of the consecrated blood.[201] Care was taken that it fell only on a favourable spot,[202] or things were so arranged that not a single drop of it was shed.[203] Sometimes, however, these precautions were considered unnecessary. At Methydrion in Arcadia the rite ordained that the victim should be torn to pieces.[204] There might even be an advantage in prolonging its agony.[205] Slow death, like sudden death, could lighten the responsibility of the sacrificer. For reasons already explained, the rituals were ingenious in discovering attenuating circumstances. The rites were simpler when only flour or cakes were sacrificed instead of an animal. The oblation was cast wholly or partially into the fire.

Through this act of destruction the essential action of the sacrifice was accomplished. The victim was separated definitively from the profane world; it was *consecrated*, it was *sacrified*, in the etymological sense of the word, and various languages gave the name *sanctification* to the act that brought that condition about. The victim changed its nature, as did Demophoon, as did Achilles, as did the son of the king of Byblos, when Demeter, Thetis, and Isis consumed their humanity in the fire.[106] Its death was like that of the phoenix:[107] it was reborn sacred. But the phenomenon that occurred at that moment had another aspect. If on the one hand the spirit was released, if it had passed completely 'behind the veil' into the world of the gods, the body of the animal on the other hand remained visible and tangible. And it too, by the fact of consecration, was filled with a sacred force that excluded it from the profane world. In short, the sacrificed victim resembled the dead whose souls dwelt at one and the same time in the other world and in the corpse. Thus its remains were treated with a religious respect:[108] honours were paid to them. The slaughter thus left a sacred matter behind it, and it was this, as we shall now see, that served to procure the useful effects of the sacrifice. For this purpose it was submitted to a double series of operations. What survived of the animal was attributed entirely to the sacred world, attributed entirely to the profane world, or shared between the two.

The attribution to the sacred world, whether to protecting divinities or to maleficent spirits, was brought about by differing procedures. One of these consisted in bringing certain parts of the animal's body into contact with the altar of the god, or with some objects which were especially consecrated to him. In the Hebrew *hattat* for Yom Kippur, as described in the opening verses of Leviticus chap. iv,[209] the sacrificer soaks his finger in the blood which is presented to him. He sprinkles it seven times before Yahweh, that is, on the veil, and smears a little blood on the horns of the altar of sweet incense, within the sanctuary.[210] The rest was poured at the foot of the altar of the *'olah* which stood at the entrance. In the ordinary *hattat* the priest smeared the blood on the horns of the altar of the *'olah*.[211] The blood of the victims of the *'olah* and the *shelamim* was simply poured out at the foot of the altar.[212] Elsewhere the sacred stone or the face of the god was daubed with it.[213] In Greece, at the sacrifices to the water-gods, the blood was allowed to flow into the water;[214] or after having been collected in a goblet, it was poured into the sea.[215] When the victim had been skinned, the idol might be dressed in the skin.[216] This rite was particularly observed in ceremonies at which a sacred animal was sacrificed, no matter what form was given to the idol.[217] In any case, the victim that had been killed was presented just as he had been presented before the consecration.[218] In the *'olah* the assistants, having cut up the victim into pieces, bear them with the head to the officiating priest, who places them upon the altar.[219] In the ritual of the *shelamim* the portions presented received significant names: *terumah*, the raised offering, *tenuphah*, the 'turned' offering.[220]

Another method was incineration. In all the Hebrew sacrifices, in the same way as the blood was completely disposed of by aspersion or effusion,[221] the fat and entrails were burned upon the altar-fire.[222] The portions thus consecrated to the god who personified the consecration accordingly reached him in a pleasant-smelling smoke.[223]

When the god intervened in the sacrifice he was considered as consuming materially and in reality the sacrificed flesh: it was 'his meat'.[114] The Homeric poems show us the gods seated at the sacrificial banquets.[115] The cooked flesh reserved for the god[116] was presented to him and set before him. The god was to consume it. In the Bible on several occasions the divine fire spurts forth and consumes the flesh lying upon the altar.[117]

From the flesh that was left over from this preliminary destruction, other portions were taken away. The priest took his share.[118] Now the share of the priest was still considered a divine share. The writers of the Pentateuch were concerned to know whether the victim of the *hattat* was to be burnt or eaten by the priests; according to Leviticus[119] Moses and the sons of Aaron were in disagreement on this point. Clearly, the two rites had thus the same meaning.[120] In the same way, in the Roman rites of expiation the priests ate the flesh.[121] In the *zebah shelamim* the priests kept for themselves the parts especially presented to Yahweh—the shoulder and the breast,[122] the *tenuphah* and the *terumah*. The portions reserved for the priests could be eaten only by them and their families, in a sacred place.[123] The Greek texts contain much information, no less precise in nature, concerning the portions of the victims and the oblations reserved for the sacrificers.[124] Sometimes, it is true, the rites appear to be not very exacting; thus the priests take their portions home with them; money is made from the skins of the victims, and the deductions come to look like perquisites. However, there is reason to believe that the priests were, in this matter also, the agents, representatives, and deputies of the god. Thus the initiates of Bacchus, when possessed, tore to pieces their victims, and devoured them.[335] Perhaps we should also consider as priestly shares various deductions made by the kings[336] or by sacred families.[337]

The purpose of the incineration and consumption by the priest was the complete elimination from temporal surroundings of the parts of the animal thus destroyed or eaten. Like the soul which had already been released by the sacrifice, they were in this way directed towards the sacred world. In some cases the destruction and consequent elimination involved the whole body and not only certain parts of it. In the Hebrew *'olah*, as in the Greek holocaust,[338] the victim was burned in its entirety upon the altar or within the sacred place, without anything being taken away from it. The priest, after washing the animal's entrails and limbs, placed them on the fire, where they were burnt up.[339] The sacrifice was sometimes called *kalil*, meaning, 'complète'.[340]

Among the cases of complete destruction some possess a special character. The immolation of the victim and the destruction of its body were effected in one single action. It was not first killed and its remains then burnt; everything took place at once. Such were the sacrifices by precipitation. Whether the animal were cast into an abyss or hurled down from the tower of a town or a temple roof[341] there was brought about *ipso facto* the brutal separation which was the sign of consecration.[342] Sacrifices of this kind were usually addressed to the infernal divinities or to evil spirits. As they were charged with evil influences, it was necessary to drive them away, to cut them off from reality. Doubtless some idea of attribution was not missing from the operation. It was vaguely imagined that the soul of the victim, with all the maleficent powers it contained, departed to return to the world of the maleficent powers; so the goat of the Atonement was dedicated to Azazel.[143] But the essential thing was to eliminate it, to drive it away. Thus there were cases of its expulsion without its being put to death. At Leucadia the escape of the victim was foreseen, but it was exiled.[144] The bird released in the fields at the sacrifice of the purification of the lepers in Judaea,[145] the βούλιμος[146] hounded from the houses and out of the city of Athens, were sacrificed in this way. In spite of ritual differences the same phenomenon takes place here as on the altar of the *'olah* at Jerusalem, when the victim disappears entirely in smoke before the face of Yahweh. In both instances it is separated and entirely disappears, although it is not towards the same regions of the religious world that it proceeds in the two cases.

When, however, the remains of the victim were not attributed wholly either to the gods or to the evil spirits, they were used to communicate either to the sacrifiers or to the objects of sacrifice the religious qualities that the sacrificial consecration had kindled within them. The operations we are about to describe correspond to those we encountered at the beginning of the ceremony. We noticed then how the sacrifier, by the laying on of hands, imparted to the victim something of his own personality. Now it is the victim or its remains which will pass on to the sacrifier the new qualities it has acquired by the action of sacrifice. This communication can be effected by a mere blessing.[147] But in general recourse was had to more material rites: for example, the sprinkling of blood[148] the application of the skin of the victim,[149] anointings with the fat,[150] contact with the residue of the cremation.[151] Sometimes the animal was cut into two parts and the sacrifier walked between them.[152] But the most perfect way of effecting communication was to hand over to the sacrifier a portion of the victim, which he consumed.[153] By eating a portion of it he assimilated to himself the characteristics of the whole. Moreover, just as there were cases when all was burnt up by the god, there were others in which the sacrifier received the whole of the oblation.[154]

However, the rights he enjoyed over the part of the victim left for him were restricted by the ritual.[155] Very often he had to consume it within a limited time. Leviticus permits the remains of a votive sacrifice (*neder*) and of the sacrifice known as *nedabah* (voluntary offering), to be eaten the day after the ceremony. But if any were left on the third day they had to be burnt; he who ate them then committed a grave sin.[156] Generally the victim must be eaten on the actual day of the sacrifice;[157] when that took place in the evening, nothing must be left till the following morning: this is the case with the sacrifice of the Passover.[158] In Greece similar restrictions were to be found, for example, in the sacrifices θεοῖς τοῖς μειλιχίοις, to the Chthonian gods, at Myonia, in Phocis.[159] Moreover, the sacrificial meal could take place only within the purlieus of the sanctuary.[160] These precautions were designed to prevent the remains of the victim, now consecrated, from coming into contact with profane things. Religion defended the sanctity of sacred objects as well as protecting the laity against their malignity. If the sanctifier, although profane, was admitted to touch and eat them, it was because the consecration which sanctified him had put him in a position to do so without danger. But the effects of his consecration lasted only for a while; after a time they disappeared, and this is why the remains had to be eaten within a set period. If what was unused was not destroyed, it had at least to be locked away and guarded.[161] Even those remains of the cremated offering that could be neither destroyed nor put to use were not thrown away at random. They were deposited in special places protected by religious prohibitions.[162]

The study of the Hindu sacrifice, the description of which we have interrupted, presents the whole gamut of all these practices—a rare instance—both those concerning attribution to the gods and those concerning communication to the sacrifiers.

Immediately after the victim has been choked to death its sacrificial purity is assured by a special rite. A priest leads up to the recumbent carcase the wife of the sacrifier, who has been present at the ceremony.[163] While the body undergoes several washings she proffers the waters of purification[164] at each orifice of the animal for it to 'drink'. When this has been done the cutting-up of the carcase begins. At the first stroke of the knife blood flows. This is allowed to run away. It is the share allotted to the evil spirits: 'Thou art the share of the *rakshas*'.[165]

Then there follows the ceremony whose purpose is to attribute to the god the essential part of the victim: this is the *vapa*—in medical parlance, the larger epiploic sac.[166] It is removed swiftly, with all sorts of precautions and propitiations. It is taken away in procession like a victim, with the sacrifier always holding on to the priest who is carrying it.[167] It is cooked over the sacred fire and so arranged that the melting fat falls drop by drop on the fire. It is said to fall upon 'the skin of the fire',[168] of Agni. Since Agni is entrusted with the task of handing over the offerings to the gods, this is a first portion attributed to them.[169] Once the *vapa* has been cooked and cut up, it is thrown into the fire,[170] amid blessings

and bowings, and after the necessary invocations have
been made. It is a second portion for the gods. This further attribution is itself considered as a kind of complete
sacrifice.[271] In this way apologies are made to the *vapa*,
just as they had been made to the victim at the moment
of sacrifice. This done, they return to the animal, which
is skinned and from which eighteen morsels[272] of flesh
are cut off and then cooked together. The fat, the meat
stock and scum[273] that float[274] on the surface in the
cooking vessel are for the god or pair of gods to whom the
sacrifice is addressed. All this is sacrificed in the fire.
What is thus destroyed again formally represents the
victim in its entirety,[275] and by this means another total
elimination of the animal is carried out. Finally, from the
eighteen pieces of meat used to make this broth, a certain
number are set aside and again attributed to various
divinities or mythical personages.[276]

But seven of these portions are used for a completely
different purpose:[277] it is through them that the sacred
strength of the victim will be passed on to the sacrifier.[278]
They constitute what is called the *ida*. This name is also
that of the goddess who personifies the animals and who
is the dispenser of good fortune and fertility.[279] The same
word thus designates this divinity and the sacrificial
portion.[280] This is because the goddess comes and incarnates herself in it during the actual course of the ceremony. The way in which this incarnation takes place is
as follows: In the hands of a priest, which have been
anointed beforehand,[281] the *ida* is placed, and the other
priests and the sacrifier surround him and touch it.[282]
While they are in this posture the goddess is invoked.[283]
Here an invocation in the literal and technical sense of
the word is meant (*vocare in*=to call into). The divinity

is not only invited to be present at and to participate in
the sacrifice, but even to descend into the offering. What
takes place is a veritable transubstantiation. On hearing
the appeal the goddess arrives, bringing with her all
kinds of mythical powers—those of the sun, the wind, the
atmosphere, the heavens, the earth, animals, etc. Thus,
as one text puts it, there is used up on the *ida* (the sacrificial portion) everything good in the sacrifice and in the
world.[284] Then the priest who held it in his hands eats
his portion,[285] after which the sacrifier does the same.[286]
Everyone remains seated in silence until the sacrifier has
rinsed his mouth.[287] Then[288] their portions are distributed to the priests, each of whom represents a god.[289]

Having made a distinction in the various rituals just
compared between the rites of attribution to the gods and
the rites of utilization by men, it is important to realize
the analogy between them. Both are made up of the
same practices and imply the same proceedings. We have
discerned in both the sprinkling of blood; the applying
of the skin, in the one case either to the altar or to the
idol, in the other to the sacrifier or the objects of sacrifice; the communion of food, fictional and mythical so far
as the gods are concerned, but real as concerns men.
Fundamentally these different operations are all sub-
stantially identical. Once the victim has been sacrificed
it is a question of placing it in contact either with the
sacred world or with the persons or things that are to
benefit from the sacrifice. The sprinkling, the touching,
and the applying of the skin are clearly only different
ways of establishing a contact that the communion of food
carries to the utmost extreme of intimacy. It brings
about not only a mere external proximity, but a mingling
of the two substances which become absorbed in each

other to the point of becoming indistinguishable. And if these two rites are similar to this extent, it is because the object pursued in the one and the other case is itself not unanalogous. In both cases it is to pass on the religious power that successive consecrations have accumulated in the object sacrificed—on the one hand to the religious sphere, in the other to the profane one to which the sacrifier belongs. Both systems of rites contribute, each in its own way, to the establishment of that continuity which appears to us, after this analysis, to be one of the most remarkable characteristics of sacrifice. The victim is the intermediary through which the communication is established. Thanks to it, all the participants which come together in sacrifice are united in it; all the forces which meet in it are blended together.

But there is something more: not only a resemblance, but a close solidarity exists between these two kinds of practices of attribution. The first kind are the condition of the second. For the victim to be used by men, the gods must have received their share. It is indeed charged with such sanctity that the profane person, in spite of the preliminary consecrations which have to some extent raised him above his ordinary and normal nature, cannot touch it without danger to himself. Consequently this religiosity which it possesses, and which makes it unusable by mere mortals, must to some degree be diminished. The immolation had already partially accomplished this. It was in the spirit that this religiosity was most highly concentrated. Once, then, the spirit has departed, the victim becomes more approachable; it can be handled with fewer precautions. There were even sacrifices in which, from then onwards, all danger had disappeared; they were those in which the whole animal was used by the sacrifier, without any part of it being attributed to the gods. But in other cases this first operation did not suffice to uncharge the victim as much as was necessary. Thus a fresh beginning had to be made, in order to eliminate even more that part which still remained too much to be feared, by driving it off into the regions of the sacred. It was necessary, as the Hindu ritual says, to perform a kind of new sacrifice.[110] This was the purpose of the rites of attribution to the gods.

Consequently the numerous rites which are practised on the victim can, in their essentials, be summed up in a simple schema. The victim is first consecrated. Then the forces which this consecration have aroused and concentrated on it are allowed to escape, some to the beings of the sacred world, others to the beings of the profane world. The series of states through which it passes might thus be represented by a curve: it rises to a maximum degree of religiosity, where it remains only for a moment, and then progressively descends. We shall see that the sacrifier passes through corresponding phases.[111]

THE EXIT

The useful results of the sacrifice have been accomplished; all, however, is not over. The group of people and things formed for the occasion around the victim has no further reason to exist. Yet it must be dissolved slowly, without disturbance, and, since it has been created through rites, it is rites alone that can unloosen the elements of which it is composed. The bonds that joined priests and sacrifier to the victim have not been broken by the act of sacrifice. All those who have shared in the sacrifice have acquired a sacred character that isolates them from the world of the profane. Yet they must be able to return to it. They must step outside the magic circle in which they remain enclosed. Moreover, during the ceremonies errors may have been committed that must be wiped out before the threads of normal life are taken up again. The rites by which this exit from the sacrifices is effected are the exact counterparts of those we observed at the entry.[292]

In the Hindu animal sacrifice, as moreover in all sacrifices according to the same ritual, this last phase of the sacrifice is very exactly set out. Sacrifice is made of what remains of the butter, and the fat is spattered on the turf.[293] Then a certain amount of equipment is destroyed in the sacrificial fire,[294] the sacrificial turf,[295], the reciter's wand, the boards that surround the *vedi*.[296] The unused lustration water is poured away and then, after due reverence has been paid to the stake,[297] a libation is made over it. Sometimes it is carried off home, for it is supposed to purify from ritual errors; or, like the turf, it is burnt.[298] All that remains of the offerings is destroyed by fire, and the utensils are cleansed and taken away after having been washed.[299] Only the spit used to roast the heart is buried—a special case in the rite, according to which the instrument of crime or of suffering must be hidden.[300]

As for the participants, this is what happens to them. The priests, the sacrifier and his wife assemble together and purify each other by the washing of hands.[301] The rite has a dual purpose: first, it purifies them from the errors that may have been committed during the sacrifice, and secondly from those that it was the object of the sacrifice to wipe out. In reality the religious atmosphere of the sacrifice is abandoned. This is what is expressed in the rite of the abandonment of the vow:[302] 'O Agni, I have made my vow, I have made good my vow, I become a man again. . . . I descend once more from the world of the gods into the world of men.'[303]

A more extreme form of the same rite will make its meaning more apparent: this is known as 'the bath of bearing away'[304] which ends the sacrifice of the *soma*, and is the opposite of the *diksha*. After the instruments have been laid aside, the sacrifier bathes in a calm pool formed by running water.[305] All that remains of the sacrifice is plunged into the water, all the pulpy branches of the *soma*.[306] The sacrifier then unties the sacrificial girdle that he had put on at the *diksha*. He unlooses also the clasp that fastened certain parts of the woman's clothing, as well as the turban, the skin of the black antelope, and the two sacrificial garments, and immerses them all. Then his wife and he, immersed up to the neck in the water, recite prayers as they bathe, washing first each other's back and then the limbs.[307] This done they emerge from the water and put on brand-new clothes.[308] Thus everything has passed into the water and thereby lost any dangerous or even simply religious character. The ritual errors that may have been made are expiated, as well as the crime that has been committed by killing Soma the god. Though this rite is more complex than that first mentioned, it is nevertheless of the same kind: facts and theory assign to it the same function.

The Biblical texts are unfortunately less complete and less clear, yet we find in them a few allusions to the same practices. At the festival of the Atonement, after having driven away the goat of Azazel, the high priest returned to the sanctuary and took off his sacred garb, 'in order not to spread abroad the consecration'. He then washed himself, put on fresh clothing, went out and sacrificed the *'olah*.[309] The man who had led away the goat bathed and washed his clothes before returning;[310] the one who had burnt the remains of the *hattat* did the same.[311] We do not know whether the other sacrifices were accompanied by similar practices.[312] In Greece, after the expiatory sacrifices, the sacrificers, who refrained as much as possible from touching the victim, washed their garments in a river or spring before returning to the town or to their homes.[313] The utensils that had been used in the sacrifice were carefully washed, when they were not destroyed.[314] These practices limited the effects of the consecration. They are important enough to have survived in the Christian Mass. After the communion the priest washes out the chalice and washes his hands. When this has been done the Mass is finished, the cycle of ceremonies is closed, and the celebrant pronounces the final formula of dismissal: *Ite, missa est*. These ceremonies correspond to those which marked the entry into the sacrifice. The faithful and the priest are liberated, just as they had been prepared at the beginning of the ceremony. They are the reverse ceremonies, they counterbalance those at the beginning.

The religious condition of the sacrifier thus also describes a curve symmetrical to the one traced by the victim. He begins by rising progressively into the religious sphere, and attains a culminating point, whence he descends again into the profane. So each one of the creatures and objects that play a part in the sacrifice is drawn along as if in a continuous movement which, from entry to exit, proceeds along two opposing slopes. But if the curves thus described have the same general contour, they do not all rise to the same height. It is of course the curve described by the victim that reaches the highest point.

It is moreover clear that the respective importance of these phases of ascent and descent can vary infinitely according to the circumstances. This will be shown in the pages that follow.

Chapter Three

HOW THE SCHEME VARIES ACCORDING TO THE GENERAL FUNCTIONS OF THE SACRIFICE

IN WHAT HAS GONE BEFORE we have indeed constructed only one scheme. But this scheme is something other than a mere abstraction. We have seen that it was realized *in concreto* in the case of the Hindu animal sacrifice. Moreover, around this rite we have been able to group a whole number of sacrificial rites that are prescribed in the Semitic ritual and in the Greek and Latin rituals. In reality, it constitutes the common material from which the more particular forms of sacrifice are taken. According to the end sought, according to the function it is to fulfil, the parts of which it is composed can be arranged in different proportions and in a different order. Some can assume more importance to the detriment of others; some may even be completely lacking. Hence arises the multiplicity of sacrifices, but without there being specific differences between the various combinations. It is always the same elements that are differently grouped or developed unequally. We shall attempt to demonstrate this by considering a few fundamental types.

The General Functions of the Sacrifice

Since the sacrifice has as its purpose to affect the religious state of the sacrifier or the object of sacrifice, we can foresee *a priori* that the general lines of our plan must vary according to what that state is at the beginning of the ceremony. Let us suppose first that it is neutral. The sacrifier—and what we say about the sacrifier could be repeated for the object of sacrifice in the case of an objective sacrifice—is not invested with any sacred character before the sacrifice. Sacrifice, therefore, has the function of imparting it to him. This is notably what occurs in sacrifices of initiation and ordination. In these cases the distance is great between the point of departure of the sacrifier and the point which he is to attain. Thus the ceremonies of introduction are necessarily very much elaborated. He enters cautiously, step by step, into the sacred world. Conversely, as the consecration is then more desired than feared, one would be afraid of lessening it by limiting and circumscribing it too closely. The sacrifier, even when he has returned to the profane world, must retain something of what he has acquired during the course of the sacrifice. Therefore the practices of the exit are reduced to their simplest expression; they may even disappear completely. The Pentateuch indicates them only when it describes the rites of the ordination of the priests and Levites. In the Christian Mass they survive only in the form of additional purifications. Moreover, the changes effected by these sacrifices are more or less of long duration. They are sometimes constitutional and imply a real metamorphosis. It was claimed that the man who touched the flesh of the human victim sacrificed to Zeus Lykaios (the *wolf*) on the Lyceum was himself changed into a wolf, just as Lycaon had been after having sacrificed a child.[215] It is even for this reason that these sacrifices are to be found in the rites of initiation, rites whose purpose is to introduce a soul into a body.[316] In any case the sacrifier, at the end of the ceremony, was endowed with a sacred character, which sometimes entailed special prohibitions. This character might even be incompatible with others of the same kind. Thus at Olympia the man who, after having sacrificed to Pelops, ate the flesh of his victim, had not the right to sacrifice to Zeus.[317]

This first characteristic goes with another. The purpose of the whole rite is to increase the religiosity of the sacrifier. To this end he had to be associated as closely as possible with the victim, because it is thanks to the strength that the act of consecration has built up in the victim that he acquires this desired characteristic. In this case, we may say that the characteristic whose transmission is the very aim of the sacrifice *passes from the victim to the sacrifier* (or to the object). Consequently, it is after the immolation that they are brought into contact, or at least it is at that moment that the most important contact is effected. Of course it may be that by the laying on of hands a bond is established between the sacrifier and the victim before the latter is destroyed. But sometimes—for example in the *zebah shelamim*—this is completely lacking, and in any case it is secondary. The most essential thing is what takes place once the victim's spirit has departed. It is then that the communion of food is practised.[318] Sacrifices of this kind might be termed sacrifices of 'sacralization'. The same word is also appropriate to sacrifices whose effect is not to create out of nothing a sacred character in the sacrifier, but simply to accentuate that sacred character of which he is already possessed.

But, not unusually, the man who is about to sacrifice already has a sacred character, from which ritual prohibitions may result which may be contrary to his intentions. The impurity[319] that he acquires by not observing religious laws or by contact with impure things is a kind of consecration.[320] The sinner, just like the criminal, is a sacred being.[321] If he sacrifices, the sacrifice has as its aim, or at least as one of its aims, to rid him of his impurity. It is an expiation. But an important fact must be noted: sickness, death, and sin are identical from the religious viewpoint. Most ritual errors are punished by misfortune or physical hurt.[322] And, reciprocally, these mischances are supposed to be caused by faults committed consciously or unconsciously. The religious consciousness, even that of our contemporaries, has never clearly dissociated the breach of the divine laws from the material consequences for the guilty person's body, his situation, and his future in another world. Thus we can treat together curative sacrifices and those that are purely expiatory. Both have it as their purpose to communicate to the victim, by the sacrificial continuity, the sacrifier's religious impurity and with that victim to eliminate it.

Thus the most elementary form of expiation is elimination pure and simple. The expulsion of Azazel's goat, and that of the bird in the sacrifice for the purification of a leper, is of this kind. On the Day of Atonement, two goats were chosen. The high priest, after various *hattat*, laid both his hands on the head of one of them, confessed over it the sins of Israel, then sent it forth into the desert. It bore away with it the sins that had been passed on to it by the laying on of hands.[323] In the sacrifice for the purification of the leper,[324] the sacrificer took two turtledoves. He cut the throat of one of them over an earthenware jar containing spring water. The other dove was dipped in this water diluted with blood, with which the leper was sprinkled. The living turtle-dove was then released and flew away, carrying the leprosy with it. The sick man had then only to make an ablution to be purified and cured. The *hattat* demonstrates as clear a procedure of elimination in cases where the remains of the victim were carried outside the camp and burned in their entirety.[315] The Hindu medicinal sacrifices reveal similar cases.[316] To cure a person of jaundice,[317] yellow birds were tied beneath the patient's bed. He was sprinkled with water in such a way that the water fell upon the birds, which began to twitter. As is said in the magic hymn, it is from this moment that the 'jaundice' is 'in the yellow birds'.[318] Let us go a little further than this too material phase of the rite; let us consider the case of a man under an evil spell. A series of rites are used, some of which are purely symbolic,[319] but others are comparable to sacrifice. To the left leg 'of a black cockerel'[320] is tied a hook, and to the hook a cake. As the bird is set free,[321] is said, 'Fly away from here, evil omen,[322] remove yourself from here; fly off elsewhere to the one who hates us; with this iron hook we bind you.'[323] The taint in the sacrifier has been attached to the bird and has disappeared with it, either by being destroyed or by falling upon the enemy.[324]

There is one case in particular, however, where it can be clearly seen that the characteristic eliminated in this way is essentially a religious one: it is that of the 'spit-ox',[325] an expiatory victim to the god Rudra. Rudra is lord of the animals, who can destroy them, and men, by plague and fever. Thus he is the dangerous god.[326] Now

as the god of cattle he exists within the herd at the same
time as he prowls round it and threatens it. To drive him
from the cattle he is concentrated in the finest bull of the
herd. This bull becomes Rudra himself; it is raised up,
consecrated as such, and homage is paid to it.[337] Then—
at least according to certain schools of opinion—it is
sacrificed outside the village, at midnight, in the woods.[338]
In this way Rudra is eliminated.[339] The Rudra of the
animals had departed to join the Rudra of the woods, the
fields, and the crossroads. Thus the purpose of the sacrifice has indeed been the expulsion of a divine element.

In all these cases the sacred character which is passed
on by sacrifice proceeds not from victim to sacrifier,[340]
but on the contrary from sacrifier to victim. It is got rid
of by being passed on to the victim. Thus it is before and
not after the act of immolation that contact between the
two takes place—at least that contact which is really
essential. Once this character has been passed on to the
victim it tends on the other hand to flee from it, as well
as from the whole environment in which the ceremony
has taken place. Because of this, rites of exit were
developed. The rites of this nature that we have indicated
in the Hebrew ritual have been presented to us only for
expiatory sacrifices. After the first sacrifice that has purified him, the leper must complete his purification by an
additional ablution and even by a new sacrifice.[341] On the
other hand, the rites of entry are limited or even missing.
The sacrifier, being already invested with a religious
character, has no need to acquire one. The religiosity that
marks him diminishes progressively from the inception
of the ceremony. The movement 'upwards' that we
found in the complete sacrifice is rudimentary or even
entirely lacking. We are thus confronted with another

type, into which enter the same elements as in the sacrifice of sacralization. But these elements are orientated in an opposite direction and their respective importance is reversed.

In what has so far been said, we have supposed that the sacred character with which the sacrifier was marked at the beginning of the sacrifice was for him a blemish, a cause of religious inferiority, sin, impurity, etc. But there are cases where the mechanism is exactly the same but where the initial state is a source of superiority for the sacrifier, constituting a state of purity. The *nazir*[842] at Jerusalem was an absolutely pure being. He had consecrated himself to Yahweh by taking a vow, in consequence of which he abstained from wine and from cutting ûs hair. He had to keep himself free from all stain. But once he had reached the end of the period of his vow,[843] he could release himself from it only by sacrifice. To do this he takes a bath of purification,[844] then he offers a lamb as '*olah*, a ewe as *hattat*, and a ram as *zebah shelamim*. He shaves his head, and throws the hair on the fire on which the meat of the *shelamim*[845] is being cooked. When the sacrificer performs the *zebah shelamim* he places on the hands of the nazir the *terumah* and the *tenuphah*, that is the consecrated portions, and a cake of the corresponding offering.[846] Afterwards these oblations are presented to Yahweh. Then, says the text, the nazir will be able to drink wine—that is to say, he is freed from his consecration. This has passed partly into the hair that is cut off and offered up on the altar, partly into the victim that represents him. Both things are eliminated. The process is thus the same as in expiation. The sacred character proceeds from the sacrifier to the victim, however high its religious value may be. Consequently the sacrifice of expiation is itself only a special variety of a more general type, which is independent of the favourable or unfavourable character of the religious state affected by the sacrifice. This might be termed the *sacrifice of desacralization.*

Things, like persons, may be in a state of such great sanctity that because of it they become unusable and dangerous. Sacrifices of this kind become necessary. This is particularly the case with the products of the earth. Each species of fruit, cereal, and other products is sacred in its entirety, forbidden, so long as a rite, often of a sacrificial nature, has not rid it of the prohibition which protects it.[347] To effect this there is concentrated in one portion of the species of the fruit all the power contained in the others. Then this part is sacrificed, and by virtue of this alone, the others are released.[348] Or again, it passes through two successive stages of desacralization: the whole of the consecration is first of all concentrated in the firstfruits, then these firstfruits themselves are represented by a victim who is eliminated. This is what happened, for example, when the first fruits were brought to Jerusalem.[349] The inhabitants of a locality[350] came in a body, bringing their baskets. At the head of the procession walked a flute player. *Kohanim* went on ahead of the oncoming people. In the town everybody stood as they passed by in order to pay due honour to the sacred things there present. Behind the flautist was a bullock, with gilded horns and crowned with olive. This bullock, who perhaps carried the fruits or drew the cart, was later sacrificed.[351] Having arrived at the holy mountain, everyone, 'even King Agrippa in person', took up his basket and walked up to the parvis.[352] The doves that were perched on it served as burnt-offerings,[353] and what was carried in the hand was handed over to the priest. Thus in each case two means were superimposed upon each other to rid the firstfruits of holiness: consecration in the temple, sacrifice of the bullock, and sacrifice of the doves, personifications of the virtues considered to inhabit them.

The comparison just made between the case of the nazir and individual expiation, between the case of the firstfruits and that of other things which must be rid of a religious character more truly evil, leads us to an important observation. It is already a remarkable fact that, in a general way, sacrifice could serve two such contradictory aims as that of inducing a state of sanctity and that of dispelling a state of sin. Since it is composed of the same elements in both cases, there cannot exist between these two states the clear-cut opposition that is generally seen. But we have also just seen that two states, one of perfect purity, the other of impurity, could be the occasion for the same sacrificial procedure, in which the elements are not only identical, but arranged in the same order and moving in the same direction. Conversely, moreover, it can happen that in certain conditions a state of impurity is treated as if it were the opposite state. This is because we have only distinguished, at the same time as the elementary mechanisms, types of an almost abstract nature, which in reality are usually interdependent. It would not be quite exact to represent expiation as an elimination pure and simple, in which the victim played merely the part of a passive intermediary or repository. The victim of the expiatory sacrifice is more sacred than the sacrifier. There is laid upon it a consecration not always different from that which it acquires in the sacrifices of sacralization. Thus we shall

see rites of sacralization and expiatory rites combined in
one and the same sacrifice. The power that the victim
contains is of a complex nature: in the Hebrew ritual the
remains of the cremation of the red heifer, which are
collected in a purified place, make a man who is in a
normal state impure by their contact, and yet serve to
purify those who have acquired certain blemishes.[354]
To the same order of facts belong certain of the contacts
established between the sacrifier and the victim after the
sacrificial slaughter: there are expiatory sacrifices in
which, after the skin of the victim has been removed, the
sacrifier must stand on or touch it before being completely
purified. In other cases the skin of the victim is dragged
to the place for which the expiation is being made.[355] In
more complex sacrifices, of which we shall have occasion
to speak later, the elimination is complicated by a process
of absorption. In short, considering carefully the Hebrew
sacrifice, the consecration of the victim is carried out in
the same way in the *hattat* and the *'olah*. The rite of
attribution of the blood is merely more complete in the
former sacrifice. And it is remarkable that, the more complete the attribution of the blood, the more perfect the
expiatory exclusion. When the blood was carried into the
sanctuary the victim was treated as impure and was burnt
outside the camp.[356] In the opposite case, the victim was
eaten by the priests like the consecrated portions of the
shelamim. What difference was there then between the
impurity of the victim of the first *hattat* and the sacred
character of the victim of the second? None—or rather
there was a theological difference between the expiatory
sacrifices and the sacrifices of sacralization. In the *hattat*
and in the other sacrifices there was indeed an attribution
of blood at the altar, but the altar was divided by a red

59

line. The blood of the *hattat* was poured out beneath the line; the blood of the burnt-offering, above it.[557] Two religious functions were present, but the distinction between them was not very profound.

This is indeed because, as Robertson Smith has clearly shown, what is pure and what is impure are not mutually exclusive opposites; they are two aspects of religious reality. The religious forces are characterized by their intensity, their importance, their dignity; consequently they are separated. That is what makes them what they are, but the direction in which they are exerted is not necessarily predetermined by their nature. They can be exerted for good as well as for evil. It depends on the circumstances, the rites employed, etc. Thus is explained the way in which the same mechanism of sacrifice can satisfy religious needs the difference between which is extreme. It bears the same ambiguity as the religious forces themselves. It can tend to both good and evil; the victim represents death as well as life, illness as well as health, sin as well as virtue, falsity as well as truth. It is the means of concentration of religious feeling; it expresses it, it incarnates it, it carries it along. By acting upon the victim one acts upon religious feeling, directs it either by attracting and absorbing it, or by expelling and eliminating it. Thus in the same way is explained the fact that by suitable procedures these two forms of religious feeling can be transformed into each other, and that rites which in certain cases appear contradictory are sometimes almost indistinguishable.

Chapter Four

HOW THE SCHEME VARIES ACCORDING TO THE SPECIAL FUNCTIONS OF THE SACRIFICE

WE HAVE JUST DEMONSTRATED how our scheme is varied to adapt itself to the different religious states in which the person affected by the sacrifice, be he who he may, finds himself. But we have not concerned ourselves with discovering what this person was in himself, but merely whether or not he possessed a sacred character before the ceremony. It is easy to predict, however, that the sacrifice cannot be the same when it is performed on behalf of the sacrifier himself or of a thing in which he has a special interest. Then the functions that it fulfils must become specialized. Let us see what differences come about on this score.

We have called those sacrifices personal that directly concern the person of the sacrifier himself. From this definition it follows that these all have one prime characteristic in common: since the sacrifier is the beginning and the end of the rite, the act begins and finishes with him. It is a closed cycle about the sacrifier. Of course, we certainly know that there is always at least an attribution of the spirit of the thing sacrificed to the god or to the religious power that operates in the sacrifice. But the fact remains that the act accomplished by the sacrifier is of direct benefit to him.

Secondly, in all these kinds of sacrifice the sacrifier, by the end of the ceremony, has improved his lot, either because he has eradicated the evil to which he was a prey, or because he has regained a state of grace, or because he has acquired a divine power. There are even numerous rituals in which a special formula, either at the exit or at the solemn moment of consecration, gives expression to this change, the salvation that is wrought[358] or the way in which the sacrifier is transported into the world of life.[359] It may even happen that the communion brings about a kind of alienation of the personality. By eating the sacred thing, in which the god is thought to be immanent, the sacrifier absorbs him. He is possessed by him, κάτοχος ἐκ τοῦ θεοῦ γίνεται,[360] just as was the priestess of the temple of Apollo on the Acropolis of Argos when she had drunk the blood of the sacrificed lamb. It would seem, it is true, that expiatory sacrifice might not have the same effect. But in reality the 'Day of Atonement' is also the 'day of God'. It is the day when those who escape from sin by sacrifice are inscribed 'in the book of life'.[361] As in the case of sacralization, the link between the sacred and the sacrifier, which is established through the victim, regenerates the sacrifier and gives him a new power. By the very fact that sin and death have been eliminated, favourably disposed forces come into play on behalf of the sacrifier.

This regeneration through personal sacrifice has given rise to some important religious beliefs. Firstly, we must link with it the theory of rebirth by sacrifice. We have

seen the symbols which identify the *dikshita* with a
foetus, then a Brahmin and a god. We know the importance of the doctrines of rebirth in the Greek mysteries, the Scandinavian and Celtic mythologies, the cult
of Osiris, the Hindu and Avestan theologies, and even in
Christian dogma. Now very often these doctrines are
linked distinctly with the accomplishment of certain
sacrificial rites: the consuming of the cake at Eleusis, of
the *soma*, of the Iranian *haoma*, etc.[302]

Often a change of name marks this re-creation of the
individual. We know that in religious belief the name is
closely linked with the personality of him who bears it:
it contains something of his soul.[303] Now sacrifice is
accompanied fairly frequently by a change of name. In
some cases this change is restricted to the addition of an
epithet. In India, even today, one may bear the title of
dikshita.[304] But sometimes the name is completely
changed. In the early Church the neophytes, after having
been exorcized, were baptized on Easter Day. Then, after
this baptism, they were given communion, and a new
name was bestowed upon them.[305] In Jewish practice
even today the same rite is employed when one's life is in
danger.[306] Now it is probable that this was formerly
accompanied by sacrifice. We know that at the moment
of agony an expiatory sacrifice was offered by the Jews,[307]
as moreover in all the religions of which we have adequate knowledge.[308] It is therefore natural to think that
both change of name and expiatory sacrifice formed part
of the same complex of ritual, giving expression to the
radical modification that is brought about at that moment
in the person of the sacrifier.

This vitalizing power of sacrifice is not limited to life
here below, but is extended to the future life. In the

course of religious evolution the notion of sacrifice has been linked to ideas concerning the immortality of the soul. On this point we have nothing to add to the theories of Rohde, Jevons, and Nutt on the Greek mysteries,[369] with which must be compared the facts cited by S. Lévi taken from the teachings of the Brahmanas,[370] and those that Bergaigne and Darmesteter had already gleaned from the Vedic[371] and Avestan[372] texts. The relationship that connects Christian communion with everlasting salvation[373] must also be mentioned. However important these facts may be, their importance must not be exaggerated. So long as the belief in immortality is not disentangled from the crude theology of sacrifice it remains vague. It is the 'non-death' (*amritam*) of the soul that is ensured by sacrifice. It is a guarantee against annihilation in the other life as well as in this. But the idea of personal immortality has only been divorced from the preceding one after a philosophical elaboration, and moreover the concept of another life does not have its origins in the institution of sacrifice.[374]

The number, variety, and complexity of objective sacrifices are such that we can only deal with them rather summarily. Save for the agricultural sacrifice, the study of which is now fairly well advanced, we shall have to content ourselves with general remarks that show how these sacrifices are linked to our general scheme.

The typical characteristic of objective sacrifices is that by definition, the chief effect of the rite accrues to some object other than the sacrifier. Indeed, the sacrifice does not return to its point of departure; the things that it aims at modifying lie outside the sacrifier. The effect produced upon him is thus secondary. Consequently, the rites of entry and exit, which are concerned particularly with the sacrifier, become rudimentary. It is the middle stage, the consecration, which tends to occupy more room. Above all else, spirit must be created,[375] whether to attribute it to the real or mythical being that the sacrifice concerns, or so that something may be freed from some sacred power that made it unapproachable, or, on the other hand, to transform this power into pure spirit—or to pursue both purposes at the same time.

But moreover, the special nature of the object whose interests are concerned in the sacrifice modifies the sacrifice itself. In the building sacrifice,[376] for example, one sets out to create a spirit who will be the guardian of the house, altar, or town that one is building or wants to build, and which will become the power within it.[377] Thus the rites of attribution are developed. The skull of the human victim, the cock, or the head of the owl, is walled up. Again, depending on the nature of the building, whether it is to be a temple, a town, or a mere house, the importance of the victim differs. According as the building is already built or is about to be built, the object of the sacrifice will be to create the spirit or the protecting divinity, or to propitiate the spirit of the soil which the building operations are about to harm.[378] The colour of the victim varies accordingly: it is, for example, black if the spirit of the earth has to be propitiated, white if a favourable spirit is to be created.[379] The rites of destruction are themselves not identical in the two cases.

In the sacrifice of request, it is sought above all to bring about certain special effects defined in the rite. If the sacrifice is the fulfilment of a promise already made, if it is carried out to release the promiser from the moral and religious bond that binds him, the victim has to some extent an expiatory character.[380] If on the other hand it is sought to bind the god by a contract, the sacrifice has rather the form of an attribution:[381] *do ut des* is the principle, and consequently no portion is set aside for the sacrifiers. If it is desired to thank the divinity for a special favour,[382] the burnt-offering—that is to say the total attribution—or the *shelamim*—the sacrifice in which a portion is left over for the sacrifier—may be mandatory. On the other hand, the importance of the victim is in direct proportion to the gravity of the vow. In short, the special characteristics of the victim depend on the nature of the thing desired: if rain is sought, one sacrifices black cows,[383] or interposes into the sacrifice a black horse on which water is poured,[384] etc. A very plausible reason can be given for this principle. As in the magical act with which these rites are in certain respects bound up, the rite acts fundamentally by itself. The force unleashed is an effective one. The victim is moulded on the votive formula, is incorporated in it, fills and animates it, bears it up to the gods, becomes its spirit, its 'vehicle'.[385]

We have only sketched out how the theme of sacrifice varies according to the different effects that it is designed to obtain. Let us see how the various mechanisms we have distinguished can be combined in one single sacrifice. From this point of view the agrarian sacrifices are excellent examples. For, though in essence objective, they have nevertheless considerable effects upon the sacrifier.

These sacrifices have a double object. Firstly, they are destined to allow the land to be worked and its products utilized, by lifting the prohibitions that protect them. Secondly, they are a means of fertilizing the cultivated fields, and of preserving their life when after the harvest they appear stripped and dead. In fact, the fields and their products are considered as eminently alive. There resides in them a religious principle that slumbers in winter, reappears in spring, is manifested in the harvest, and thus makes harvest difficult for mortals to enter upon. Sometimes this principle is even represented as a spirit that mounts guard over the earth and its fruits. It possesses them, and it is this possession that constitutes their sanctity. It must therefore be eliminated in order that the harvest and the use of the crops be made possible. But at the same time, since it is the very life of the field, after having been expelled it must be recreated and fixed in the earth whose fertility it produces. The sacrifices of simple desacralization may be adequate for the first need, but not for the second. Thus, for the most part agrarian sacrifices have a multiplicity of effects. In them different forms of sacrifice are found combined. This is one of the cases where we observe best that fundamental complexity of sacrifice which we cannot over-emphasize. Thus we do not claim, in these few pages, to present a general theory of agrarian sacrifice. We do not venture to foresee all the apparent exceptions, and we cannot unravel the tangle of historical developments. We shall confine ourselves to the analysis of a well-known sacrifice which has already been the object of a number of studies. This is the sacrifice to Zeus Polieus which the Athenians celebrated at the festival known by the name of *Diipolia* or *Bouphonia*.[386]

This festival[387] took place in the month of June, at the end of the harvest and the beginning of the corn-threshing season. The chief ceremony took place on the Acropolis at the altar of Zeus Polieus. Cakes were laid on a bronze table. They were unguarded.[388] Then bullocks were let loose. One of them approached the altar, ate a

portion of the offerings, and trampled the rest under-
foot.[***] Immediately one of the sacrificers struck it with
his axe. When it was brought to the ground, a second
sacrificer finished it off by slitting its throat with a knife.
Others flayed it, while the one who had struck the first
blow took flight. After the judgement at the Prytaneion
which we have already mentioned, the flesh of the
bullock was shared among those present, the skin, after
having been filled with straw, was sewn up again, and
the stuffed animal was harnessed to a plough.

These singular practices gave rise to legend. Three
different versions attributed it to three different personages: one to Diomos, the priest of Zeus Polieus, another to
Sopatros, the third to Thaulon;[***] these seemed indeed
to be the mythical ancestors of the priests of this sacrifice.
In all three versions the priest lays the offering upon the
altar; a bullock approaches and appropriates it; the furious
priest strikes the sacrilegious animal and, now sacrilegious himself, goes into exile. The longest of these
versions is the one in which Sopatros is the hero. A
drought and a famine result from his crime. When the
Pythian oracle is consulted, she tells the Athenians that
the exiled priest could save them. The murderer must be
punished, the victim brought back to life in a sacrifice
similar to the one in which it died, and its flesh eaten.
Sopatros is brought back, his rights are restored to him so
that he may offer up the sacrifice, and the festival is
celebrated as described.

Such are the facts: what do they mean? In this festival
three actions must be distinguished: (i) the death of the
victim, (ii) the communion, (iii) the victim's resurrection.[***]

At the beginning of the ceremony cakes and seeds are

68

laid upon the altar. These are probably the firstfruits of the threshed corn.[3][4][1] This oblation is similar to all those which allow the profane to use the harvest. All the sanctity of the corn to be threshed has been concentrated in the cakes.[3][4][3] The bullock touches them. The suddenness of the blow that strikes it demonstrates that, like a lightning flash, consecration has passed over it. It has embodied the divine spirit immanent in the firstfruits it has eaten. It becomes that spirit, so much so that its slaughter is a sacrilege. The victim of the agrarian sacrifice always represents symbolically the fields and their products. Thus it is brought into contact with them before the final conservation. In the present instance the bullock eats the cake made of the firstfruits, in others it is led through the fields or the victim is killed with agricultural implements or half-buried.

But the facts must be considered in another light. The victim, as well as the field, can also represent the devotees who are about to profane the harvest by putting it to use.[3][4][4] Not only did the products of the earth cause the sacrifier to go away, he could even be in such a condition that he had to remain away from them. The sacrifice was to remedy that condition. In certain cases purificatory practices took place during the ceremony. Thus a confession was linked to the sacrifice.[3][4][5] At other times the sacrifice itself effected this kind of expiation. It could be considered as a real redemption. In this way the Passover became a general rite of redemption on the occasion of the eating of the firstfruits. Not only was the life of the first-born[3][4][6] among men redeemed by the blood of the Paschal lamb,[3][4][7] but every Hebrew was also freed from danger. These facts might perhaps be compared with the contests that took place between the sacrifiers at certain agrarian festivals.[398] The blows appeared to sanctify, purify, and redeem them. Thus, in the first moment of the rite,[399] a double action takes place: (i) the desacralization of the harvested and threshed corn by means of the victim which represents it; (ii) the redemption of the harvest-women and the ploughmen by the immolation of this victim, who represents them.

For the Diipolia, the documents do not allude to a communication taking place between the sacrifier and the victim before the consecration. But it does occur afterwards: it is realized in a communion meal[400] which constitutes a new phase in the ceremony. After the sacrificers have been absolved from their sacrilege those present may dare to take communion. We recall that, according to the myth, the Pythian oracle had advised them to do so.[401] A large number of agrarian sacrifices are followed by a similar kind of communion.[402] By virtue of this communion the sacrifiers of the Diipolia shared in the sacred nature of the victim. They received a form of consecration that was modified, because it was shared and because a portion of the bullock remained intact. Invested with the same sacred character as the things they wished to use, they could approach them.[403] It is by a rite of this character that the Kaffirs of Natal and Zululand, at the beginning of the year, permit themselves to use the new fruits; the flesh of a victim is cooked with seeds, fruits, and vegetables. The king places a little in the mouth of each man, and this communion sanctifies him the whole year through.[404] The communion of the Passover had the same result.[405] Very often, in the sacrifices celebrated before the ploughing, the ploughman is given a portion of the victim's flesh.[406] It is true that this communion may appear to be useless, since the preliminary sacrifice has already had the effect of profaning the earth and the seeds. It seems to have had a dual use,[407] and it is indeed possible that sometimes the communion sufficed to bring about the effect desired. But it generally follows upon a desacralization, which already produces a first profanation. This is very noticeable in the Hindu rite of the *Varunapraghasas*. The barley is consecrated to Varuna,[408] it is his food.[409] The myth relates that formerly the creatures that partook of it became dropsical. It is through the rite of which we are about to speak that they escaped this danger.[410] It is performed as follows. Among other offerings,[411] two priests make from grains of barley two figurines in the form of a ram and a ewe lamb. The sacrifier and his wife place on the ewe and the ram respectively tufts of wool that represent breasts and testicles, in as great a quantity as possible.[412] Then the sacrifice is performed; a portion is attributed to Varuna, as well as other offerings of barley. Then the rest is solemnly eaten. Varuna, 'through the sacrifice, is driven away'[413] and is eliminated. Those who eat the barley are freed from the 'bond' with which he might bind them. Then, by eating the remains of the figurines, the very spirit of the barley is absorbed. The communion is thus clearly superadded to the desacralization. In this and similar cases, it is doubtless feared that the profanation has not been complete, and, moreover, that the sacrifier has received only a semi-consecration. The sacrifice establishes a balance between the sanctity of the object to be brought into use and that of the sacrifier.

But in sacrifices whose purpose is to fertilize the earth,[414] that is, to infuse into it a divine life, or to render more active the life it may possess, there is no longer question, as before, of eliminating from it a sacred character. One must be communicated to it. Thus the processes of direct or indirect communication are necessarily involved in operations of this kind. A spirit that will make it fertile must be fixed in the soil. The Khonds sacrificed human victims to ensure the fertility of the earth. The flesh was shared out among the different groups and buried in the fields.[415] Elsewhere the blood of the human victim was sprinkled over the earth.[416] In Europe ashes are spread on the fields on the feast of St John, blessed bread on the feast of St Antony,[417] the bones of animals at Easter and other festivals.[418] But often the whole of the victim was not used in this way, and, as at the Bouphonia, the sacrifiers received their share.[419] Sometimes it was even attributed to them in its entirety. It was a way of allowing the ploughman to share in the benefits of consecration, and perhaps even to entrust to his charge the forces that he assimilated to himself, and which, in other cases, were fixed in the field. Moreover, the remnants of the meal were sown later, when it came to sowing or ploughing time.[420] Or indeed a fresh victim was shared out, a new incarnation of the agrarian spirit, and the life that had formerly been drawn from the earth was disseminated in it once more. What was given back to the earth was what had been borrowed from it.[421] This fundamental correspondence between the rites of profanation of the firstfruits and those of the fertilization of the fields, between the two victims—this could in certain cases give rise to a veritable fusion of the two ceremonies, which were then practised on the same victim. This is what happened at the Bouphonia. These are a sacrifice with a dual aspect: they are a sacrifice of the threshing, since they began by an offering of the firstfruits, but they have also as their ultimate purpose the fertilization of the earth. Indeed, we have seen that according to the legend the festival was established so as to put a stop to a famine and a drought. It might even be said that the communion carried out by using the bullock's flesh has likewise this dual purpose: to allow the consumption of the new grain, and to bestow a special blessing on the citizens for their future agricultural tasks.

But let us continue with our analysis of the data. We arrive at the third phase of our rite. Sopatros, by killing the bullock, had killed the spirit of the corn, and the corn had not grown again. According to the terms of the oracle, the second sacrifice must bring the dead victim back to life. This is why the dead bullock is stuffed with straw; the stuffed bullock[412] is the bullock brought back to life. It is harnessed to the plough. The imitation 'ploughing' that it is made to carry out over the fields corresponds to the dispersal of the victim among the Khonds. But it must be noticed that the individual existence of the bullock and of its spirit survives both the eating of its flesh and the diffusion of its sacredness. This spirit, which is the very same that has been extracted from the harvest when reaped, is to be found again in the skin sewn up after having been filled with straw. This characteristic is not peculiar to the Bouphonia. In one of the Mexican festivals, to represent the rebirth of the spirit of agriculture the dead victim was skinned and the skin put on the victim that was to succeed it the following year.[413] In Lusatia, at the spring festival, in which the 'dead one', the old god of vegetation, is buried, the shirt from the manikin that represents it is removed and immediately placed on the May tree;[414] with the garment, the spirit

73

is also removed. It is thus the victim itself that is reborn. Now this victim is the very spirit of vegetation, which, at first concentrated in the firstfruits, was then carried over into the animal, and has, moreover, been purified and rejuvenated by the immolation. It is thus the very principle of germination and fertility; it is the life of the fields that is in this way reborn and revivified.[415]

What is especially striking in this sacrifice is the unbroken continuity of this life whose duration and transmission it ensures. Once the spirit has been released by the sacrificial slaughter, it remains fixed in the place to which the rite has directed it. In the Bouphonia it resides in the manikin of the stuffed bullock. When the resurrection was not represented by a special ceremony, the preservation of a part of the victim or of the oblation attested to the persistence and presence of the spirit that resided within it. In Rome not only was the head of the October horse preserved, but its blood also was kept until the Palilia.[416] The ashes of the sacrifice of the Forcidiciae were likewise kept until that time.[417] In Athens the remains of the pigs sacrificed at the Thesmophoria[418] were stored away. These relics served as a body for the spirit released by the sacrifice. They allowed it to be seized and used, but—and this first of all—to be preserved. The periodical return of the sacrifice at times when the earth became bare assured the continuity of natural life. It permitted the localizing and fixing of the sacred character that it was advantageous to preserve, and which reappeared the following year in the new fruits of the soil, to be incarnated again in a fresh victim.

The succession of agrarian sacrifices thus presents an unbroken series of concentrations and diffusions. As soon as the victim has become a spirit, a genius, it is shared out, it is dispersed, so that life may be sown with it. So that this life may not be lost—and there is always risk of losing a little of it, as witness the story of Pelops and his ivory shoulder—it must from time to time be brought together again. The myth of Osiris, whose scattered limbs were reassembled by Isis, is an image of this rhythm and alternation. In short, the sacrifice contained in itself the condition of its recurrence, not taking into account the regular recurrence of the labour of the fields. Moreover, this is laid down in the legend that records the institution of these sacrifices. The Pythian oracle prescribed the indefinite repetition of the Bouphonia, and other ceremonies of the same kind. Any interruption was inconceivable.

In a word, just as personal sacrifice ensured the life of the person, so the objective sacrifice in general and the agrarian sacrifice in particular ensure the real and healthful life of things.

Yet generally the ceremonial of the agrarian sacrifices, one type of which we have just analysed, has been overlaid with ancillary rites, or even distorted according to the interpretation that has been put on certain of its practices. Magical rites of rain and sun are generally mixed up with it: the victim is drowned, or water is poured upon it; the fire of sacrifice or special fires represent the fire of the sun.[419] On the other hand, it could happen that when the rites of desacralization, whether of object or sacrifier, predominated, the whole rite could take on the character of a true expiatory sacrifice,[420] as Frazer has shown. The spirit of the fields that came out of the victim took on the form of a scapegoat.[421] The agrarian festival became a festival of Atonement. In Greece the myths that recorded the institution of these festivals often represented them as the periodical expiation of original crimes. Such is the case with the Bouphonia.[411]

Thus from one single agrarian sacrifice a whole body of consequences may emerge. The value of the victim of a solemn sacrifice was so great, the expansive force of the consecration so wide, that it was impossible to limit its efficacy in an arbitrary fashion. The victim was a centre of attraction and radiated influences from it. The things that the sacrifice could attain received their share of these influences. According to the condition, nature, and needs of persons or objects, the effects produced could differ.

Chapter Five

THE SACRIFICE OF THE GOD

THIS SINGULAR VALUE OF THE VICTIM clearly appears in one of the most perfected forms of the historical evolution of the sacrificial system: the sacrifice of the god. Indeed, it is in the sacrifice of a divine personage that the idea of sacrifice attains its highest expression. Consequently it is under this guise that it has penetrated into the most recent religions and given rise to beliefs and practices still current.

We shall see how the agrarian sacrifices were able to provide the point of departure for this evolution. Mannhardt and Frazer[411] already saw clearly the close connexions between the sacrifice of the god and the agrarian sacrifices. We shall not recapitulate those points of the topic that they have already dealt with. But, with the help of some additional facts, we shall seek to show how this form of sacrifice is linked to the very essence of the mechanism of sacrifice. Our main efforts will be especially directed towards determining the considerable part that mythology has played in this development.

In order that a god may thus descend to the role of a victim, there must be some affinity between his nature and that of his victims. So that he may come to submit himself to destruction by sacrifice, his own origins must be in the sacrifice itself. In certain respects this condition appears to be fulfilled in all sacrifices, for the victim has

always something divine within it which is released by
sacrifice. But a divine victim is not a victim-god.⁴⁸⁴ The
sacred character that encompasses religious things must
not be confused with those clearly defined personages, the
object of myths and rites equally clearly defined, who are
called gods. In objective sacrifices, it is true, we have
already seen that there are released from the victim
entities whose traits were more definite because they
were linked to a definite object and function. In the building sacrifice it may even be the case that the spirit created
is almost a god. Yet these personages of myth generally
remain vague and blurred. It is above all in the agrarian
sacrifices that they are most clearly determined. They owe
this distinction to various causes.

Firstly, in these sacrifices the god and the victim that is
sacrificed are specially homogeneous. The spirit of a
house is something other than the house it protects. The
spirit of the corn, on the other hand, is almost indistinct
from the corn that embodies it. To the god of the barley
are offered victims made from the barley in which the
god resides. We may therefore anticipate that, as a consequence of this homogeneity and the fusion that results
from it, the victim will be able to communicate its own
individuality to the spirit. So long as it remains merely
the first sheaf of the harvest or the firstfruits of the crop,
the spirit, like the victim, remains something essentially
agrarian.⁴⁸⁵ Thus it leaves the fields only to return to
them immediately. It does not become concrete until the
precise moment when it is concentrated in·the victim. As
soon as it is immolated, it is diffused once more through
the entire agrarian species to which it gives life, and so
again becomes vague and impersonal. For its personality
to become more marked, the links that bind it to the

fields must be weakened, and for this the victim itself must be joined less closely to the things that it represents. A first step along this road is taken when, as often happens, the consecrated sheaf receives the name or even the form of an animal or man. Sometimes even, as if to make the transition more apparent, a living animal is trussed up inside it,[436]—a cow, a goat, or a cock, for example, which becomes the harvest cow, goat, or cock. Thus the victim loses a part of its agrarian nature, and to the same extent the spirit becomes detached from what has sustained it. This independence is further increased when the sheaf is replaced by an animal victim. Then the connexion with what it embodies becomes so remote that it is sometimes difficult to perceive. Only by comparison has it been discovered that the bull and the goat of Dionysus, the horse and the pig of Demeter, were incarnations of the life of the corn and the vine. But the differentiation becomes specially apparent when the part is assumed by a man,[437] who brings to it his own autonomy. Then the spirit becomes a moral person who has a name, who begins to have an existence in legend apart from festivals and sacrifices. In this way the spirit of the life of the fields gradually becomes exterior to the fields[438] and is individualized.

But to this first cause another is added. Sacrifice, of itself, effects an exaltation of the victims, which renders them directly divine. There are numerous legends in which these apotheoses are related. Herakles was not admitted to Olympus until his suicide on Oeta. Attis[439] and Eshmun[440] were animated after death with a divine life. The constellation of Virgo is none other than Erigone, an agrarian goddess who hanged herself.[441] In Mexico a myth relates that the sun and moon were created by a sacrifice.[443] The goddess Toci, mother of the gods, was also presented as a woman whom sacrifice made divine.[443] In the same country, at the festival of the god Totec, prisoners were killed and flayed, and a priest donned the skin of one of them and became the image of the god. He wore the god's ornaments and garb, sat on a throne, and received in his place the images of the first-fruits.[444] In the Cretan legend of Dionysus, the heart of the god, who had been slaughtered by the Titans, was placed in a *xoanon*, where it was worshipped.[445] Philo of Byblos uses a very significant expression to describe the state of Okeanos, mutilated by his son Kronos: 'he was consecrated', ἀφιερώθη.[446] In these legends subsists a vague consciousness of the power of sacrifice. A vestige persists also in the rites. At Jumièges, for example, where the part of the annual vegetation spirit was taken by a man whose tenure of office lasted for a year from Mid-summer Day, a pretence was made of casting the future *loup vert* into the log fire. After this simulated execution his predecessor handed over to him his insignia of office.[447] The ceremony did not have as its effect merely to embody the spirit of agriculture; the spirit was born in the sacrifice itself.[448] Now, given that we cannot distinguish between evil spirits and agrarian victims, these facts are precisely examples of what we have stated concerning consecration and its direct effects. The sacrificial apotheosis is none other than the rebirth of the victim. Its divinization is a special case and a superior kind of sanctification and separation. But this form hardly occurs save in sacrifices where, by localizing, concentrating, and accumulating a sacred character, the victim is invested with the highest degree of sanctity—a sanctity organized and personified in the sacrifice.

This is the necessary condition for the sacrifice of the god to be possible. But in order that it may become a reality, it is not enough for the god to have emerged from the victim. He must still possess his divine nature in its entirety at the moment when he enters again into the sacrifice to become a victim himself. This means that the personification from which he has resulted must become lasting and necessary. This indissoluble association between creatures or a species of creatures and a supernatural power is the fruit of the regular recurrence of the sacrifices, which is here in question. The repetition of these ceremonies in which, as a result of a habit or for any other reason, the same victim reappears at regular intervals has created a kind of continuous personality. Since the sacrifice preserves its secondary effects, the creation of the divinity is the work of previous sacrifices. And this is no chance, irrelevant fact, since, in a religion as abstract as Christianity, the figure of the Paschal Lamb, the customary victim of an agrarian or pastoral sacrifice, has persisted and still serves even today to designate Christ, that is to say God. Sacrifice has furnished the elements of divine symbolism.

But it is the imagination of the creators of myths which has perfected the elaboration of the sacrifice of the God. Indeed, imagination has given firstly a status and a history and consequently a more continuous life to the intermittent, dull, and passive personality, which was born from the regular occurrence of sacrifices. This is without taking into account the fact that by releasing it from its earthly womb, it has made it more divine. Sometimes we can even follow in the myth the various phases of this progressive divinization. Thus the great Dorian

festival of the Karneia, celebrated in honour of Apollo
Karneios, was instituted, it was related, to expiate the
murder of the soothsayer Karnos, slain by the Heraclid
Hippotes.[449] Now Apollo Karneios is none other than the
soothsayer Karnos whose sacrifice is accomplished and
expiated like that of the Diipolia. And Karnos himself, 'the
horned one',[450] becomes confused with the hero Krios,
'the ram',[451] the hypostasis of the original animal victim. From the sacrifice of the ram mythology had created
the murder of a hero and afterwards transformed this
latter into a great national god.

But, though mythology has elaborated the representation of the divine, it has not worked upon arbitrary facts.
The myths preserve traces of their origin: a sacrifice in
more or less distorted form constitutes the central episode
and, so to speak, the heart of the legendary life of the
gods that arose from sacrifice. Sylvain Lévi has explained
the part that sacrificial rites play in Brahmanic mythology.[452] Let us see how, more especially, the history of
the agrarian gods is woven on to a backcloth of agrarian
rites. To demonstrate this we will group together some
types of Greek or Semitic legends, resembling those of
Attis and Adonis, which are so many distortions of the
theme of the sacrifice of the god. Some are myths that
explain the institution of certain ceremonies, others are
tales generally arising from myths similar to the former.[453] Often the commemorative rites that correspond
to these legends (sacred dramas, processions, etc.)[454]
have, so far as we know, none of the characteristics of
sacrifice. But the theme of the sacrifice of the god is a
motif which mythological imagination has freely used.

The tomb of Zeus in Crete,[455] the death of Pan,[456]
and that of Adonis are well enough known for a mere

mention of them to suffice. Adonis has left in Syrian legend descendants who share his fate.[487] It is true that in some cases the divine tombs are perhaps monuments of the cult of the dead. But more frequently, in our opinion, the mythical death of the god recalls the ritual sacrifice. It is wrapped up in the legend, which is otherwise obscure, handed down in a garbled form and incomplete as to circumstances that might allow us to determine its true nature.

On the Assyrian tablet of the legend of Adapa we may read:[488] 'From the earth have disappeared two gods; this is why I wear the garb of mourning. Who are these two gods? They are Du-mu-zu and Gish-zi-da.' The The death of Du-mu-zu is a mythical sacrifice. This is proved by the fact that Ishtar, his mother and wife, wishes to bring him back to life[489] by pouring over his corpse water from the spring of life, which she has fetched from hell—for in this she imitates the rites of certain agrarian feasts. When the spirit of the fields has died or has been put to death, its body is thrown into the water or is sprinkled with water. Then, whether it is restored to life or whether a May tree rises up above its tomb, life is reborn. Here it is the water poured over the corpse, and the resurrection, which cause us to identify the dead god with an agrarian victim. In the myth of Osiris it is the dispersal of the corpse and the tree which grows on his coffin.[490] At Troezen, in the peribolum of the temple of Hippolytus, an annual festival commemorated the λιθοβόλια, the death of the goddesses Damia and Auxesia, virgins and strangers from Crete, who according to tradition had been stoned in a revolt.[491] The foreign goddesses are the stranger, the passer-by who often plays a part in the festivals of the harvest; the

stoning is a rite of sacrifice. Often the mere wounding of
a god is equivalent to his yearly death. Belen, asleep in
the Blumenthal at the foot of the rounded mountain top
of Guebwiller, was wounded in the foot by a wild boar,
just as Adonis was, and from every drop of blood that
flowed from his wound sprang up a flower.[443]

The death of the god is often by suicide. Herakles on
Oeta, Melkart at Tyre,[444] the god Sandes or Sandon at
Tarsus,[445] Dido at Carthage—all burnt themselves to
death. The death of Melkart was commemorated each
summer by a festival which was a festival of the harvest.
Greek mythology has goddesses who bore the name of
'Απαγχομένη, the 'hanged' goddesses: such were Artemis,
Hecate, and Helen.[446] At Athens the hanged goddess
was Erigone, the mother of Staphylos, the hero of the
grape.[447] At Delphi she was called Charila.[447] Charila,
the story went, was a little girl who during a famine had
gone to the king to ask him for her share of the last
distribution of food. Beaten and driven away by him, she
had hanged herself in an isolated valley. Now an annual
festival was celebrated in her honour, instituted, it was
said, by the Pythian oracle. It began with a distribution
of corn. Then an image of Charila was made; it was
beaten, hung, and buried. In other legends the god
inflicts upon himself some mutilation from which he
sometimes dies. Such is the case with Attis and with
Eshmun, who pursued by Astronoe, mutilated himself
with an axe.

It was often the founder of a cult or the chief priest
of the god whose death was related in the myth. Thus at
Iton, Iodama, on whose tomb burnt a sacred fire, was the
priestess of Athena Itonia.[448] In the same way Aglauros
of Athens, whose death the Plynteria were supposed to

expiate, was also the priest of Athena. In reality the priest and the god are but one and the same person. Indeed we know that the priest can be an incarnation of the god as well as the victim: often he disguises himself in the god's likeness. But here there is the first differentiation, a sort of mythological doubling of the divine being and the victim.[469] Thanks to this doubling the god appears to escape death.

It is to a differentiation of another kind that those myths are due whose central episode is a god's combat with a monster or another god. In Babylonian mythology such are the fights of Marduk with Tiamat, that is to say with Chaos;[470] those of Perseus killing the Gorgon or the dragon of Joppa, of Bellerophon struggling against the Chimera, of St. George vanquishing the Dajjal.[471] This is also the case with the labours of Herakles, and indeed with all theomachies, for in all these contests the vanquished is as divine as the conqueror.

This episode is one of the mythological forms of the sacrifice of the god. These divine struggles are indeed equivalent to the death of a single god. They alternate in the same festivals.[472] The Isthmian games, celebrated in spring, commemorate either the death of Melikertes or the victory of Theseus over Sinis. The Nemean games celebrate either the death of Archemoros or the victory of Herakles over the Nemean lion. They are sometimes accompanied by the same incidents. The defeat of the monster is followed by the marriage of the god, of Perseus with Andromeda, of Herakles with Hesione. The betrothed who is a prey to attack by the monster and is delivered by the hero is moreover none other than the 'May Bride' of German legend, pursued by the spirits of the wild hunt. In the cult of Attis the sacred marriage follows the death and resurrection of the god. They are brought about in analogous circumstances and have the same purpose. The victory of a young god over an age-old monster is a rite of spring. The festival of Marduk, on the first day of Nisan, re-enacted his victory over Tiamat,[473] The festival of St. George, that is, the defeat of the dragon, was celebrated on 23 April.[474] Now it was in the spring that Attis died. Lastly, if it is true, as Berossus reports, that an Assyrian version of the Genesis story showed Bel cutting himself in two to give birth to the world, the two episodes appear concurrently in the legend of the same god: the suicide of Bel replaces his duel with Chaos.[475]

To complete the proof of this equivalence of themes, it must be added that the god often dies after his victory. In Grimm (*Märchen*, 60) the hero is assassinated when asleep after his struggle with the dragon; the animals who accompany him recall him to life.[476] The legend of Herakles displays the same adventure: after having slain Typhon, Herakles lay lifeless, asphyxiated by the monster's breath; he was only restored to life by Iolaos, with the help of a quail.[477] In the legend of Hesione, Herakles was swallowed by a whale. Castor, after having killed Lynkeus, was himself slain by Idas.[478]

These equivalences and alternations are easily explicable if we consider that the opponents brought face to face by the theme of combat are the product of the doubling of a single spirit. The origin of myths of this form has generally been forgotten. They are presented as meteorological combats between the gods of light and those of darkness or the abyss,[479] the gods of heaven and those of hell. But it is extremely difficult to distinguish clearly the character of each of the contestants. They are beings of the same nature, whose differentiation, accidental and fluctuating, belongs to the religious imagination. Their kinship appears fully in the Assyrian pantheon. Assur and Marduk, solar gods, are the kings of the Annunaki, the seven gods of the abyss.[400] Nergal, sometimes named Gibil, the god of fire, bears elsewhere the name of a monster of hell. As for the seven gods of the abyss, it is difficult, especially in the mythologies that succeeded the Assyrian mythology, to distinguish them from the seven planetary gods, the executors of the will of heaven.[401] Long before Greco-Roman syncretism, which made the sun the lord of Hades,[402] and compared Mithras with Pluto and Typhon,[403] the Assyrian tablets said that Marduk ruled over the abyss,[404] and that Gibil, the fire,[405] and Marduk himself are sons of the abyss.[406] In Crete the Titans who put Dionysus to death were his relatives.[407] Elsewhere the hostile gods were brothers, often twins.[408] Sometimes the struggle took place between uncle and nephew, or even between father and son.[409]

Even if this relationship is lacking, another connexion links the actors in the drama and shows their fundamental identity. The animal sacred to Perseus at Seriphos was the crab, the καρκίνος.[410] Now the crab which, in the legend of Seriphos, was the enemy of the Octopus, is allied with the Lernean hydra, who is an octopus, to fight with Herakles. The crab, like the scorpion, is now the ally, now the enemy of the sun-god. All in all, they are forms of the same god. The Mithraic bas-reliefs show Mithras riding on the bull that he is going to sacrifice. Thus Perseus rode Pegasus, sprung from the Gorgon's blood. The monster or the sacrificial animal served as a mount for the victorious god before or after the sacrifice. In short, the two gods in the struggle or the mythical

G

hunt are collaborators. Mithras and the bull, says
Porphyry, are demiurges of equal status.[401]

Thus sacrifice had produced in mythology an innumerable offspring. Passing from abstraction to abstraction, it had become one of the fundamental themes of divine legend. But it is precisely the introduction of this episode into the legend of a god which determined the shaping of a ritual for the sacrifice of the god. Priest or victim, priest and victim, it is a god already formed that both acts and suffers in the sacrifice. Nor is the divinity of the victim limited to the mythological sacrifice; it also appears in the actual sacrifice which corresponds to it. Once the myth has taken shape it reacts upon the rite from which it sprang and is realized in it. Thus the sacrifice of the god is not merely the subject of a good mythological story. Whatever changes the personality of the god may have undergone in the syncretism of pagan beliefs, whether fully developed or decayed, it is still the god who undergoes the sacrifice; he is not a mere character in it.[402] At least in the origin, there is a 'real presence', as in the Catholic mass. St Cyril of Alexandria [403] relates that in certain ritual combats of gladiators, of regular recurrence, a certain Kronos (τις Κρόνος) hidden under the earth, received the purifying blood which flowed from their wounds. This Κρόνος τις is the Saturn of the Saturnalia who, in other rituals, was put to death.[404] The name given to the representative of the god tended to identify him with the god. For this reason the high priest of Attis, who also played the part of the victim, bore the name of his god and mythical predecessor.[405] Mexican religion offers some well-known examples of the identity of victim and god. Particularly at the festival of Huitzilopochtli[406] the statue of the god, made from

beetroot paste and kneaded in human blood, was divided
into pieces, shared out among the devotees, and eaten.
Doubtless, as we have seen, in every sacrifice the victim
has something of the god in him. But here it is the god
himself, and it is this identification which characterizes
the sacrifice of the god.

But we know that the sacrifice is repeated periodically
because the rhythm of nature demands this regular
recurrence. The myth, then, shows the god emerging
alive from the test only in order to submit him to it
afresh. His life is thus composed of an uninterrupted
chain of sufferings and resurrections. Astarte brings
Adonis back to life, Ishtar Tammuz, Isis Osiris, Cybele
Attis, and Iolaos Herakles.[497] The slain Dionysus is conceived for the second time by Semele.[498] We are already
a long way from the apotheosis mentioned at the beginning of this chapter. The god emerges from the sacrifice
only to return into it, and conversely. There is no longer
any break in his personality. If he is rent in pieces, as are
Osiris and Pelops, the pieces are found, put together and
re-animated. Then the primitive purpose of the sacrifice
is relegated to the background. It is no longer an agrarian
or pastoral sacrifice. The god who comes to it as a victim
exists in himself—he has a multiplicity of qualities and
powers. From this it follows that the sacrifice appears to
be a repetition and a commemoration of the original
sacrifice of the god.[499] To the legend that relates it some
circumstance that guarantees its perpetuity is usually
added. Thus when a god dies a more or less natural death,
an oracle prescribes an expiatory sacrifice which re-
enacts the death of this god.[500] When one god vanquishes
another, he perpetuates the memory of his victory by the
inauguration of a cult.[501]

It must be noticed here that the abstraction which, in the sacrifice, caused the god to be born, could impart another aspect to the same practices. By a process analogous to the doubling which produced the theomachies, it could separate the god from the victim. In the myths studied above, the two adversaries are equally divine. One of them appears as the priest in the sacrifice in which his predecessor expires. But the virtual divinity of the victim is not always developed. Often the victim has remained earthly, and consequently the god created, who had formerly emerged from the victim, now remains outside the sacrifice. Then the consecration, which causes the victim to pass into the sacred world, takes on the appearance of an attribution or gift to a divine person. Even in this case, however, it is always a sacred animal that is sacrificed, or at least something that recalls the origin of the sacrifice. In short, the god was offered to himself: Dionysus the ram became Dionysus Kriophagos.[502] Sometimes, on the other hand, as in the doublings which resulted from the theomachies, the sacrificed animal passed for an enemy of the god.[503] If it was immolated it was to expiate a crime committed against a god by its species. To the Virbius of Nemi, slain by horses, a horse was sacrificed.[504] The notion of sacrifice *to* the god developed parallel with that of sacrifice *of* the god.

The types of sacrifice of the god which we have just reviewed are realized *in concreto* and combined together in one and the same Hindu rite, the sacrifice of the soma.[505] Firstly we can see here what in the ritual is a veritable sacrifice of the god. We cannot show here how Soma the god is confused with soma, the plant, how he is really present in it, or describe the ceremonies at which it is brought in and received at the place of sacrifice. It is carried on a shield, worshipped, then pressed and killed. Then, from these pressed branches, the god is released and spreads himself through the world. A series of distinct attributions communicate him to the various realms of nature. This real presence, this birth of the god that follows upon his death are, in a fashion, the ritual forms of the myth. As for the purely mythical forms that this sacrifice has acquired, they are indeed those we have described above. There is firstly, the identification of the god Soma with Vritra, the enemy of the gods, the evil spirit who holds the treasures of immortality and whom Indra kills.[504] For, to explain how a god can be slain, he was represented in the guise of an evil spirit. It is the evil spirit who is put to death, and from it emerges the god. From the covering of wickedness that enclosed it is released the excellent essence. But on the other hand it is often Soma who kills Vritra; in any case it is he who gives his strength to Indra, the warrior god, the destroyer of the demons. In some texts even it is Soma who is his own sacrificer. They go so far as to represent him as the archetype of the heavenly sacrificers. From this to the suicide of the god the distance is not great. This distance the Brahmins bridged.

In this way they spotlighted an important point in the theory of sacrifice. We have seen that between the victim and the god there is always some affinity: to Apollo Karneios rams are offered, to Varuna barley, etc. Like is fed to like, and the victim is the food of the gods. Thus sacrifice quickly came to be considered as the very condition of the divine existence. This it is that provides the immortal substance on which the gods live. Thus not only is it in sacrifice that some gods are born, it is by sacrifice that all sustain their existence. So it has ended by appearing as their essence, their origin, and their creator.[507] It is also the creator of things, for in it the principle of all life resides. Soma is at one and the same time the sun and the moon in the heavens, the cloud, the lightning flash and the rain in the atmosphere, the king of plants upon earth. In the soma as victim, all these forms of Soma are combined. He is the repository of all the nourishing and fertilizing principles in nature. He is at the same time the food of the gods and the intoxicating drink of men, the author of the immortality of the one, and of the ephemeral life of the others. All these forces are concentrated, created, and distributed anew by sacrifice. This then is 'the lord of beings', Prajapati. It is the Purusha[508] of the famous hymn X, 90 of the Rig-Veda, from which are born the gods, rites, men, castes, sun, moon, plants, and cattle. It will become the Brahman of classical India. All theologies have attributed to it that creative power. Scattering and combining the divinity in turn, it sows beings as Jason and Cadmus sowed the dragon's teeth from which warriors were born. From death it draws out life. Flowers and plants grow on the corpse of Adonis; swarms of bees fly out from the body of the lion killed by Samson, and from the bull of Aristaeus.

Thus theology borrowed its cosmogonies from the sacrificial myths. It explained creation by sacrifice, just as popular imagination explained the yearly life of nature. For this it traced back the sacrifice of the god to the origin of the world.[509]

In the Assyrian cosmogony, the blood of the vanquished Tiamat had given rise to creatures. The separation of the elements from chaos was looked upon as the sacrifice or suicide of the demiurge. Gunkel[510] has proved, in our view, that the same concept was to be found in the popular beliefs of the Hebrews. It appears in Nordic mythology. It is also at the basis of the Mithraic cult. The bas-reliefs set out to portray the life that springs from the sacrificed bull; its tail is shown as ending in a bunch of ears of corn. In India the continual creation of things by means of the rite eventually becomes an absolute *creatio ex nihilo*. In the beginning there was nothing. Purusha desired. It is through his suicide, by the abandonment of himself, by the renunciation of his body, later a model for the Buddhist renunciation, that the god brought about the existence of things.

We may suppose that the regular recurrence of sacrifice persisted when sacrifice was heroified at this level. The recurrent onslaughts of chaos and evil unceasingly required new sacrifices, creative and redemptive. Thus transformed and, so to speak, purified, sacrifice has been preserved by Christian theology.[511] Its efficacy has simply been transferred from the physical world to the moral. The redemptive sacrifice of the god is perpetuated in the daily Mass. We do not claim to examine here how the Christian ritual of sacrifice was built up, or how it is linked to earlier rites. We believe, however, that in the course of this work we have sometimes been able to compare the ceremonies of the Christian sacrifice with those we have studied. It must suffice here simply to recall their astounding likeness, and to indicate how the development of rites so like those of the agrarian sacrifice could give rise to the concept of a sacrifice of redemption and communion of the unique and transcendent god. In this respect the Christian sacrifice is one of the most instructive to be met with in history. By the same ritual processes our priests seek almost the same effects as our most remote ancestors. The mechanism of consecration in the Catholic Mass is, in its general form, the same as that of the Hindu sacrifices. It shows us, with a clarity leaving nothing to be desired, the alternating rhythm of expiation and communion. The Christian imagination has built upon ancient models.

Chapter Six

CONCLUSION

IT CAN NOW BE SEEN more clearly of what in our opinion the unity of the sacrificial system consists. It does not come, as Smith believed, from the fact that all the possible kinds of sacrifice have emerged from one primitive, simple form. Such a sacrifice does not exist. Of all the procedures of sacrifice, the most general, the least rich in particular elements, that we have been able to distinguish, are those of sacralization and desacralization. Now actually in any sacrifice of desacralization, however pure it may be, we always find a sacralization of the victim. Conversely, in any sacrifice of sacralization, even the most clearly marked, a desacralization is necessarily implied, for otherwise the remains of the victim could not be used. The two elements are thus so closely interdependent that the one cannot exist without the other.

Moreover, these two kinds of sacrifice are still only abstract types. Every sacrifice takes place in certain given circumstances and with a view to certain determined ends. From the diversity of the ends which may be pursued in this way arise varying procedures, of which we have given a few examples. Now there is no religion in which these procedures do not coexist in greater or lesser number; all the sacrificial rituals we know of display a great complexity. Moreover, there is no special rite that is not complex in itself, for either it pursues several ends at the same time, or, to attain one end, it sets in motion several forces. We have seen that sacrifices of desacralization and even expiatory sacrifices proper become entangled with communion sacrifices. But many other examples of complexity might be given. The Amazulu, to bring on rain, assemble a herd of black bullocks, kill one and eat it in silence, and then burn its bones outside the village; which constitutes three different themes in one operation.[512]

In the Hindu animal sacrifice this complexity is even more marked. We have found shares of the animal attributed for expiation purposes to evil spirits, divine shares put on one side, shares for communion that were enjoyed by the sacrifier, shares for the priests that were consumed by them. The victim serves equally for bringing down imprecations on the enemy, for divination, and for vows. In one of its aspects sacrifice belongs to the theriomorphic cults, for the soul of the animal is dispatched to heaven to join the archetypes of the animals and maintain the species in perpetuity. It is also a rite of consumption, for the sacrifier who has laid the fire may not eat meat until he has made such a sacrifice. Lastly it is a sacrifice of redemption, for the sacrifier is consecrated: he is in the power of the divinity, and redeems himself by substituting the victim in his place. All this is mixed up and confused in one and the same system, which, despite its diversity, remains none the less harmonious. This is all the more the case with a rite of immense purport like the sacrifice to Soma, in which, over and above what we have just described, is realized the case of the sacrifice of the god. In a word, just like a magic ceremony or prayer, which can serve at the same time as an act of thanksgiving, a vow, and a propitiation, sacrifice can fulfil a great variety of concurrent functions.

But if sacrifice is so complex, whence comes its unity? It is because, fundamentally, beneath the diverse forms it takes, it always consists in one same procedure, which may be used for the most widely differing purposes. *This procedure consists in establishing a means of communication between the sacred and the profane worlds through the mediation of a victim, that is, of a thing that in the course of the ceremony is destroyed.* Now, contrary to what Smith believed, the victim does not necessarily come to the sacrifice with a religious nature already perfected and clearly defined: it is the sacrifice itself that confers this upon it. Sacrifice can therefore impart to the victim most varied powers and thereby make it suitable for fulfilling the most varied functions, either by different rites or during the same rite. The victim can also pass on a sacred character of the religious world to the profane world, or vice versa. It remains indifferent to the direction of the current that passes through it. At the same time the spirit that has been released from the victim can be entrusted with the task of bearing a prayer to the heavenly powers, it can be used to foretell the future, to redeem oneself from the wrath of the gods by making over one's portion of the victim to them, and, lastly, enjoying the sacred flesh that remains. On the other hand, once the victim has been set apart, it has a certain autonomy, no matter what may be done. It is a focus of energy from which are released effects that surpass the narrow purpose that the sacrifier has assigned to the rite. An animal is sacrificed to redeem a *dikshita*; an immediate consequence is that the freed spirit departs to nourish the eternal life of the species. Thus sacrifice naturally exceeds the narrow aims that the most elementary theologies assign to it. This is because it is not made up solely of a series of individual actions. The rite sets in motion the whole complex of sacred things to which it is addressed. From the very beginning of this study sacrifice has appeared as a particular ramification of the system of consecration.

There is no need to explain at length why the profane thus enters into a relationship with the divine: it is because it sees in it the very source of life. It therefore has every interest in drawing closer to it, since it is there that the very conditions for its existence are to be found. But how is it that the profane only draws nearer by remaining at a distance from it? How does it come about that the profane only communicates with the sacred through an intermediary? The destructive consequences of the rite partly explain this strange procedure. If the religious forces are the very principle of the forces of life, they are in themselves of such a nature that contact with them is a fearful thing for the ordinary man. Above all, when they reach a certain level of intensity, they cannot be concentrated in a profane object without destroying it. However much need he has of them, the sacrifier cannot approach them save with the utmost prudence. That is why between these powers and himself he interposes intermediaries, of whom the principal is the victim. If he involved himself in the rite to the very end, he would find death, not life. The victim takes his place. It alone penetrates into the perilous domain of sacrifice, it dies there, and indeed it is there in order to die. The sacrifier remains protected: the gods take the victim instead of him. *The victim redeems him.* Moses had not circumcised his son, and Yahweh came to 'wrestle' with him in a hostelry. Moses was on the point of death when his wife savagely cut off the child's foreskin and, casting it at Yahweh's feet, said to him: 'Thou art for me a husband of blood.' The destruction of the foreskin satisfied the god; he did not destroy Moses, who was redeemed. There is no sacrifice into which some idea of redemption does not enter.

But this first explanation is not sufficiently general, for in the case of the offering, communication is also effected through an intermediary, and yet no destruction occurs. This is because too powerful a consecration has grave drawbacks, even when it is not destructive. All that is too deeply involved in the religious sphere is by that very fact removed from the sphere of the profane. The more a being is imbued with religious feeling, the more he is charged with prohibitions that render him isolated. The sacredness of the Nazir paralyses him. On the other hand, all that enters into a too-intimate contact with sacred things takes on their nature and becomes sacred like them. Now sacrifice is carried out by the profane. The action that it exerts upon people and things is destined to enable them to fulfil their role in temporal life. None can therefore enter with advantage upon sacrifice save on condition of being able to emerge from it. The rites of exit partly serve this purpose. They weaken the force of the consecration. But by themselves alone they could not weaken it sufficiently if it had been too intense. It is therefore important that the sacrifier or the object of sacrifice receive the consecration only when its force has been blunted, that is to say, indirectly. This is the purpose of the intermediary. Thanks to it, the two worlds that are present can interpenetrate and yet remain distinct.

Conclusion

In this way is to be explained a very particular characteristic of religious sacrifice. In any sacrifice there is an act of abnegation since the sacrifier deprives himself and gives. Often this abnegation is even imposed upon him as a duty. For sacrifice is not always optional; the gods demand it. As the Hebrew ritual declares, worship and service is owed them; as the Hindus say, their share is owed them. But this abnegation and submission are not without their selfish aspect. The sacrifier gives up something of himself but he does not give himself. Prudently, he sets himself aside. This is because if he gives, it is partly in order to receive. Thus sacrifice shows itself in a dual light; it is a useful act and it is an obligation. Disinterestedness is mingled with self-interest. That is why it has so frequently been conceived of as a form of contract. Fundamentally there is perhaps no sacrifice that has not some contractual element. The two parties present exchange their services and each gets his due. For the gods too have need of the profane. If nothing were set aside from the harvest, the god of the corn would die; in order that Dionysus may be reborn, Dionysus' goat must be sacrificed at the grape-harvest; it is the *soma* that men give the gods to drink that fortifies them against evil spirits. In order that the sacred may subsist, its share must be given to it, and it is from the share of the profane that this apportionment is made. This ambiguity is inherent in the very nature of sacrifice. It is dependent, in fact, on the presence of the intermediary, and we know that with no intermediary there is no sacrifice. Because the victim is distinct from the sacrifier and the god, it separates them while uniting them: they draw close to each other, without giving themselves to each other entirely.

There is, however, one case from which all selfish cal-
culation is absent. This is the case of the sacrifice of the
god, for the god who sacrifices himself gives himself
irrevocably. This time all intermediaries have disappeared. The god, who is at the same time the sacrifier,
is one with the victim and sometimes even with the
sacrificer. All the differing elements which enter into
ordinary sacrifice here enter into each other and become
mixed together. But such mixing is possible only for
mythical, that is, ideal beings. This is how the concept
of a god sacrificing himself for the world could be
realized, and has become, even for the most civilized
peoples, the highest expression and, as it were, the ideal
limit of abnegation, in which no apportionment occurs.

But in the same way as the sacrifice of the god does
not emerge from the imaginary sphere of religion, so it
might likewise be believed that the whole system is
merely a play of images. The powers to whom. the
devotee sacrifices his most precious possession seem to
have no positive element. The unbeliever sees in these
rites only vain and costly illusions, and is astounded that
all mankind has so eagerly dissipated its strength for
phantom gods. But there are perhaps true realities to
which it is possible to attach the institution in its entirety.
Religious ideas, because they are believed, exist; they
exist objectively, as social facts. The sacred things in relation to which sacrifice functions, are social things. And this
is enough to explain sacrifice. For sacrifice to be truly
justified, two conditions are necessary. First of all, there
must exist outside the sacrifier things which cause him
to go outside himself, and to which he owes what he
sacrifices. Next, these things must be close to him so that
he can enter into relationship with them, find in them

the strength and assurance he needs, and obtain from contact with them the benefits that he expects from his rites. Now this character of intimate penetration and separation, of immanence and transcendence, is distinctive of social matters to the highest degree. They also exist at the same time both within and outside the individual, according to one's viewpoint. We understand then what the function of sacrifice can be, leaving aside the symbols whereby the believer expresses it to himself. It is a social function because sacrifice is concerned with social matters.

On the one hand, this personal renunciation of their property by individuals or groups nourishes social forces. Not, doubtless, that society has need of the things which are the materials of sacrifice. Here everything occurs in the world of ideas, and it is mental and moral energies that are in question. But the act of abnegation implicit in every sacrifice, by recalling frequently to the consciousness of the individual the presence of collective forces, in fact sustains their ideal existence. These expiations and general purifications, communions and sacralizations of groups, these creations of the spirits of the cities give—or renew periodically for the community, represented by its gods—that character, good, strong, grave, and terrible, which is one of the essential traits of any social entity. Moreover, individuals find their own advantage in this same act. They confer upon each other, upon themselves, and upon those things they hold dear, the whole strength of society. They invest with the authority of society their vows, their oaths, their marriages. They surround, as if with a protective sanctity, the fields they have ploughed and the houses they have built. At the same time they find in sacrifice the means of redressing equilibriums that have been upset: by expiation they redeem themselves from social obloquy, the consequence of error, and re-enter the community; by the apportionments they make of those things whose use society has reserved for itself, they acquire the right to enjoy them. The social norm is thus maintained without danger to themselves, without diminution for the group. Thus the social function of sacrifice is fulfilled, both for individuals and for the community. And as society is made up not only of men, but also of things and events, we perceive how sacrifice can follow and at the same time reproduce the rhythms of human life and of nature; how it has been able to become both periodical by the use of natural phenomena, and occasional, as are the momentary needs of men, and in short to adapt itself to a thousand purposes.

Moreover we have been able to see, as we have proceeded, how many beliefs and social practices not strictly religious are linked to sacrifice. We have dealt in turn with questions of contract, of redemption, of penalties, of gifts, of abnegation, with ideas relating to the soul and to immortality which are still at the basis of common morality. This indicates the importance of sacrifice for sociology. But in this study we have not had to follow it in its development or all its ramifications. We have given ourselves only the task of attempting to put it in its place.

NOTES

ABBREVIATIONS

The following bibliographical abbreviations
are used in the Notes

AitB	*Aitareya Brahmana*
ApShS	*Apastamba Shrauta Sutra*
AshvShS	*Ashvalayana Shrauta Sutra*
AV	*Atharva Veda*
Frazer, *GB*	J. G. Frazer, *Golden Bough* (references are to first edn., 2 vols., London, 1890)
Hillebrandt, *NVO*	A. Hillebrandt, *Das Altindische Neu- und Vollmondsopfer* (Jena, 1879)
KauS	*Kaushika Sutra*
KShS	*Katyayana Shrauta Sutra*
Lévi, *Sacrifice*	Sylvain Lévi, *La Doctrine du sacrifice dans les Brahmanas* (Paris, 1898)
Mannhardt, *MythForsch*	Mannhardt, *Mythologische Forschungen* (Strasbourg, 1884)
Mannhardt, *WFK*	Mannhardt, *Wald- und Feldkulte* (Berlin, 1875–7)
Oldenberg, *RelV*	Oldenberg, *Religion der Veda* (Berlin, 1894)
Paton, *Cos*	W. R. Paton and E. L. Hicks, *The Inscriptions of Cos* (Oxford, 1891)
RV	*Rig Veda*
Schwab, *Thieropfer*	Julius Schwab, *Das altindische Thieropfer* (Erlangen, 1886)
ShB	*Shatapatha Brahmana*
Smith, *Kinship*	Robertson Smith, *Kinship and Marriage in Early Arabia* (Cambridge, 1885)
Smith, *RS*	Robertson Smith, *Religion of the Semites* (London, 1889; 2nd edn., 1894)

Stengel, *GK*	Stengel, *Die griechischen Kultusalter-thümer* (Munich, 1898)
TB	*Taittiriya Brahmana*
TS	*Taittiriya Samhita*
VS	*Vajasaneyi Samhita*
WAI	H. C. Rawlinson, *The Cuneiform Inscriptions of Western Asia* (London, 1861–70)

INTRODUCTION

1. *Primitive Culture* (London, 1871), II, ch. xviii.
2. See a rather superficial brochure by F. Nitzsch, *Die Idee und die Stufen des Opferkultus* (Kiel, 1889). Fundamentally, this is the theory adopted by the two writers who have most severely criticized Robertson Smith: Wilken, 'Eene nieuwe theorie over den oorsprong des offers', *De Gids*, 1891, Pt. III, pp. 535ff, and M. Marillier, 'La Place du totémisme . . .', *Revue d'histoire des religions*, vol. 37, 1897–8.
3. *Encyclopedia Britannica* (9th edn., 1875–80), article 'Sacrifice'; *The Religion of the Semites*.
4. J. F. McLennan, 'The Worship of Animals and Plants', *Fortnightly Review*, N.S. VI (1869), pp. 407ff, 562ff; N.S. VII (1870), pp. 194ff.
5. *Kinship and Marriage in Early Arabia*.
6. Jevons, *An Introduction to the History of Religion* (London, 1896). For its limitations see pp. 111, 115, 160. E. Sidney Hartland, *The Legend of Perseus* (London, 1894–6), II, chap. xv, adopted Robertson Smith's theory.
7. Frazer, *The Golden Bough*, chap. iii.
8. Mannhardt, *WFK*; *MythForsch*.
9. We must first of all indicate what texts we are using and what is our critical attitude towards them. The documents of the Vedic ritual are divided into Vedas or Samhitas, Brahmanas, and Sutras. The Samhitas are the collections of hymns and formulas recited during the rites; the Brahmanas are the mythological and theological commentaries on the rites; the Sutras are the ritual manuals. Though each of these orders of texts rests on another, like a series of successive strata of which the most ancient are the Vedas (see Max Muller, *History of Sanskrit Literature*, London, 1859, p. 572) we may, with the Hindu tradition which Sanskrit scholars are

tending more and more to adopt, consider them all as forming one whole and as complementary to each other. Without attributing to them precise or even approximate dates, we can assert that they are incomprehensible without each other. The meaning of thé prayers, the opinions of the Brahmins, their actions, are all closely linked, and the meaning of the facts cannot be given without a continual comparison of all the texts. These are divided up according to the functions of the priests who use them, and of the various Brahmin clans. We have used the following: 'Schools of the Narrator': the Rig Veda, a collection of hymns employed by the *hotar* (not that it contains only ritual hymns, or is of recent date), 2nd edn., Max Muller (Sacred Books of the East, vol. XXXII), translation by Ludwig; and among other texts of this school the *Aitareya Brahmana*, ed. Aufrecht, trans. (into English) by Martin Haug (Bombay, 1863); and, as Sutra, the *Ashvalayana Shrauta Sutra* (Bibliotheca Indiana, vol. 49); 'Schools of the Officiant': (a) School of the White Yajurveda (Vajasaneyins), texts ed. by Weber; *Vajasaneyi Samhita*, the Veda of formulas; *Shatapatha Brahmana*, trans. Eggeling (Sacred Books of the East, vols. XII, XXVI, XLI, XLIII, XLIV); *Katyayana Shrauta Sutra*; (b) School of the Black Yajurveda (Taittiriyas) *Taittiriya Samhita* (ed. Weber, Indische Studien, XI and XII) contains the formulas and the Brahmana; *Taittiriya Brahmana*, also contains formulas and the Brahmana; *Apastamba-shrauta-sutra* (ed. R. Garbe) whose ritual we have especially followed. To these texts must be added those of the domestic ritual, tne *Grihya Sutras* of the various schools (trans. Oldenberg in Sacred Books of the East, vols. XXIX, XXX). Besides these there is the series of Atharva texts (for the Brahmin): *Atharva-Veda*, the Veda of incantations (ed. Whitney and Roth); translations: selections by Bloomfield in Sacred Books of the East, vol. XLII; books viii–xiii, V. Henry. *Kaushika Sutra*, ed. Bloomfield. Our study of Hindu ritual would have been impossible without the works of Caland, Winternitz, and Sylvain Lévi.

For our study of sacrifice in the Bible, the basis is the Pentateuch. We shall not attempt to borrow from Biblical criticism the elements of a history of Hebrew sacrificial rites. Firstly, the materials for such a study seem to us insufficient. Next, even if we believe that Biblical criticism can provide the history of the texts, we refuse to confuse this history with that of the facts. In particular, whatever may be the date of Leviticus and of the Priestly Code in general, the age of the text is not, in our view, necessarily the age of the rite; the characteristics of the ritual may perhaps only have been settled rather late, but they existed before they were recorded. Thus we have been able to avoid posing in the case of each rite the question whether it did or did not belong to an ancient ritual. On the weakness of some of the conclusions of the critical school, see J. Halévy, 'Recherches bibliques', *Revue Sémitique* (1898), pp. 1ff, 97ff, 193ff, 289ff; (1899) 1ff. On Hebrew sacrifice see the following general works: S. Munk, *Palestine* (Paris, 1845); W. Nowack, *Lehrbuch der hebräischen Archeologie* (Freiburg, 1894), II, pp. 138ff; I. Benzinger, *Hebräische Archeologie* (Leipzig, 1894), pp. 431ff; see also the following special works: H. Hupfeld, *De prima et vera festorum apud Hebraeos ratione* (Programm, Halle, 1851); E. Riehm, 'Über das Schuldopfer', *Theologische Studien und Kritiken*, 1854; W. F. Rinck, 'Das Schuldopfer', *ibid.*, 1885; J. Bachmann, *Die Festgesetze des Pentateuchs* (Berlin, 1858); J. H. Kurtz, *Der alttestamentliche Opferkultus* (Mitau, 1862); E. Riehm, 'Der Begriff der Sühne im alten Testament', *Theologische Studien und Kritiken*, vol. 50, 1877; J. C. Orelli, 'Einige alttestamentliche Prämissen zur neutestamentlichen Versöhnungslehre', *Zeitschr. für christl. Wissen und christl. Leben*, 1884; Müller, *Kritische Versuch über den Ursprung und die geschichtliche Entwicklung des Pessach und Mazzothfestes* (Inaug. Diss., Bonn, 1884); H. Schmoller, 'Das Wesen der Sühne in der alttestamentlichen Opfertora', *Theol. Stud. und Krit.*, vol. 64 (1891); Folck, *De Nonnullis Veteris Testamenti Prophetarum Locis, etc.* (Programm, Dorpat, 1893); B. Baentsch, *Das Heiligkeitsgesetz, Lev. xvii–xxvii* (Erfurt, 1893); A. Kamphausen, *Das Verhältnis des Menschenopfers zur israelitischen Religion* (Programm, Bonn, 1896). On the Gospel texts on sacrifice, see Berdmore Compton, *Sacrifice* (London, 1896).

CHAPTER ONE

10. The *yajamana* of the Sanskrit texts. Note the use of this word, the present participle middle voice of the verb *yaj*, to sacrifice. For the Hindu writers the sacrifier is the person who expects the effect of his acts to react on himself. (Compare the Vedic formula, 'We who sacrifice for ourselves', the *ye yajamahe* of the Avestan formula *yazamaide* (Alfred Hillebrandt, *Ritual Litteratur*, Strasbourg, 1897, p. 11). These *benefits* of the sacrifice are, in our view, the necessary consequences of the rite. They are not to be attributed to the free divine will that theology has gradually interpolated between the religious act and its consequences. Thus it will be understood that we have neglected a certain number of questions

which imply the hypothesis of the sacrifice-gift, and the intervention of strictly personal gods.

11. This is normally the case with the Hindu sacrifice, which is, as nearly as possible, an individual one.

12. e.g., *Iliad* I, 313f.

13. This is particularly the case with true totemic sacrifices, and with those in which the group itself fulfils the role of sacrificer, and kills, tears apart, and devours the victim; finally, it is also the case with a good number of human sacrifices, above all those of endocannibalism. But often the mere fact of being present is enough.

14. In ancient India the master of the house (*grihapati*) sometimes sacrifices for the whole family. When he is only a participant in the ceremonies, his family and his wife (the latter is present at the great sacrifices) receive certain effects from the sacrifice.

15. According to Ezekiel, the prince (*nasi*=exilarch) had to pay the costs of sacrifice at festivals, to provide the libations and the victim. Cf. Ezek. xlv, 17; II Chron. xxxi, 3.

16. See below, p. 65.

17. See below, p. 65, n. 378. We shall cite especially the sacrifices celebrated at the entrance of a guest into the house: H. C. Trumbull, *The Threshold Covenant* (Edinburgh, 1896), pp. 1ff.

18. On the blood covenant and the way it has been linked to sacrifice, see Smith, *RS*, Lecture IX; H. C. Trumbull, *The Blood Covenant* (London, 1887).

19. On the consecration of hair, see G. A. Wilken, 'Über das Haaropfer und einige andere Trauergebräuche bei den Volkern Indonesiens', *Revue coloniale internationale*, 1884.

20. Lev. ii, 1ff; vi, 7ff; ix, 4ff; x, 12ff; Exod. xxiii, 18; xxxiv, 25; Amos iv, 5. The *minha* so far fulfils the function of any other sacrifice that a *minha* without oil and incense replaces a *hattat* and bears the same name. (Cf. Lev. v, 11). *Minha* is often used with the general meaning of sacrifice (e.g., I Kings xviii, 29, etc.). Conversely, in the Marseilles inscription the word *zebah* is applied like *minha* to vegetable oblations: *C.I.S.* 165, 1, 12; 1, 14; cf. *ibid.*, 167, li. 9 and 10.

21. Lev. ii.

22. Aristophanes, *Plutus*, ll. 659ff. Stengel, *GK*, pp. 89ff.

23. Porphyry, *De abstinentia*, ii, 29. Diogenes Laertius, viii, 13 (Delos). Stengel, *GK*, p. 92. Pliny, *Nat. Hist.*, xviii, 7. Scholium on Persius, ii, 48.

24. Smith, *RS*, pp. 230ff. He sees even in the libations of wine and oil of the Semitic rituals equivalents of the blood of animal victims.

25. K. Bernhardi, *Trankopfer bei Homer*, Programm des königlichen Gymnasiums zu Leipzig, 1885. H. von Fritze, *De libatione veterum Graecorum*, Berlin, 1893.

26. νηφάλια and μελίκρατον. See Stengel, *GK*, pp. 93 and 111. J. G. Frazer, *Pausanias* (1898), III, p. 583.

27. Stengel, *GK*, p. 99. A libation of spirits has sometimes replaced, in modern practice, the ancient sacrifices. See P. Bahlmann, *Münsterlandische Märchen* (Münster, 1898), p. 341. Cf. Paul Sartori, 'Über das Bauopfer', *Zeitschr. für Ethnologie*, vol. 30 (1898), p. 25.

28. See the texts cited by A. Hillebrandt, *NVO*, pp. 42, 43.

29. Were these vegetable offerings substituted for bloody sacrifices, as was implied in the Roman formula, *in sacris simulata pro veris accipi* (Servius, *Ad Aeneid.*, II, 116; Festus, 360b)? It was doubtless convenient to imagine a steady progress from human to animal sacrifice, then from animal sacrifice to figurines representing animals, and thence, finally, to the offering of cakes. It is possible that in certain cases, which moreover are little known, the introduction of new rituals brought about these substitutions. But there is no authority for applying these facts to make generalizations. The history of certain sacrifices presents rather a reverse process. The animals made from dough that were sacrificed at certain agricultural festivals are images of agrarian evil spirits and not simulacra of animal victims. The analysis of these ceremonies later will give the reason for this.

30. It follows from this definition that between religious punishment and sacrifice (at least, expiatory sacrifice) there are both analogies and differences. Religious punishment also implies a consecration (*consecratio bonorum et capitis*); it is likewise a destruction and is wrought by this consecration. The rites are similar enough to those of sacrifice for Robertson Smith to have seen in them models of expiatory sacrifice. Only, in the case of punishment, the manifestation in a violent fashion of the consecration affects directly the one who has committed the crime and who is himself expiating it; in the case of expiatory sacrifice, on the other hand, substitution takes place, and it is upon the victim, and not upon the guilty one, that expiation falls. However, as society is contaminated by the crime, the punishment is at the same time a means for it to rid itself of the contamination with which it is sullied. Thus, in respect of society, the guilty one fulfils the part of an expiatory victim. It may be said that there is punishment and sacrifice at one and the same time.

Notes

31. See Max Muller, 'Die Todtenbestattung bei den Brahmanen', *Zeitschrift der Deutschen Morgenländischen Gesellschaft*, vol. IX, p. lxiii. *KShS*, 1. 2. 10, 12, and commentary of Mahidhara, *ad loc.*, esp. at 11. Cf. Kulluka on Manu, 2, 25. *Vedanta Sara*, 7ff (ed. Böhtlingk in *Sanskrit-Chresto.*, pp. 254, 255). It appears that this classification is adhered to only by fairly recent authorities, while others go back to more ancient texts. But in fact it is to be found firstly in the liturgical collections which distinguish from the regular formulas (*yajus*) the formulas of the optional rites (*kamyeshtiyajyas*) and those of the expiatory rites (*prayashcittani*). It is to be found in the Brahmanas (for example, the *TB*) which devote very long sections either to expiations or to special vows and necessary sacrifices. Finally, the sutras continually separate the rites into constant (*nityani*), obligatory, and periodic, into optional (*kamyani*), occasional (*naimittikani*), and expiatory (*prayashcittani*). These divisions are to be found in the solemn as well as the domestic ritual. (See Oldenberg, 'Survey of the Contents of the Grihyasutras', in Sacred Books of the East, vol. XXX, pp. 306ff.) These texts also contain passages concerning the curative rites (*bhaishajyani*) parallel to those made known to us in the *Kaushika Sutra* (Adh. III, ed. Bloomfield, 1890). Thus the sacrifices were indeed divided according to this classification from the very beginning, although it did not become a conscious division until later.

32. The *vajapeya*. A. Weber, 'Über den Vajapeya', *Sitzber. k. k. Akad. d. Wiss. zu Berlin, Phil.-hist. Kl.* (1892), pp. 765ff, and A. Hillebrandt, *Vedische Mythologie* (Breslau, 1891–1902), I, p. 247.

33. For example, in order to obtain a son or long life (Hillebrandt, *Ritual Litteratur* (see n. 10 above), sects. 58 and 66). These sacrifices are extremely numerous, more so indeed than the published texts which present them to us.

34. The principle is even so rigorous that the ritual of sacrifice is laid down even before that of the setting up of the altar. (See Hillebrandt, *ibid.*, sect. 59, Vorbemerkung.)

35. Hillebrandt, *ibid.*, sect. 66.

36. We thus translate the word *soma*, in the composite form *somayajna*, as a common noun. The term is untranslatable, for the word designates at the same time the plant as the victim, the god released by the sacrifice, and the god sacrificed. Subject to this consideration, we make our own choice.

37. In fact the *soma* cannot be sacrificed except at the time when it is in flower, that is, the spring. (See *Ashvalayana soma prayoga* in MS Wilson 453, Oxford, Bodleian Library, fo. 137.)

Notes

38. There is indeed the greatest possible analogy between the ritual of the sacrifice of the animal at Agni-Soma (*ApShS*, VII) and the Atharvan ritual of the smothering to death of the vasha (sterile cow) (*KauS*, 44 and 45). Similarly, in the domestic ritual the various animal sacrifices, including that of the expiatory bull (see below, p. 55) are so analogous to each other that both, according to different schools of thought, were able to serve as the fundamental theme for the description (see Hillebrandt, *Ritual Litteratur* (see n. 10 above), sect. 44).

39. Deut. xii, 6, 11, 27, cf. Levit. xvii, 8, cf. Judg. xx, 26, II Sam. vi, 17, etc., mention only the '*olah* and the *zebah* or *shelamim*. The question of discovering whether these passages relate to previous rituals or to parallel ones is not important for the special purpose of our work. For the theory according to which the expiatory sacrifices were only introduced into the Hebrew ritual at a later date, see the summary of Benzinger, *Hebräische Archeologie*, pp. 441 and 447ff. The passage I Sam. iii, 14 is too vague for us to be able to conclude from it in any way against the existence of the *hattat*. In any case it is impossible to admit that expiatory sacrifices are transformations of a monetary fine.

40. Levit. iv, 2.

41. *Shelamim=zebah shelamim*. On the equivalence of the *zebahim* and the *zebah shelamim*, see Benzinger, *ibid.*, p. 435.

42. In translating the word '*olah* we adhere to the traditional interpretation, which is moreover founded on the Biblical phrase 'he caused the '*olah* to rise up (the rising up)'. Cf. Clermont-Ganneau, 'L'Inscription Nabatéenne de Kanathat', *Comptes-Rendus de l'Académie des Inscriptions*, Paris, Series 4, vol. 26, 1898, p. 599. For the '*avon* and its expiation, see Halévy in *Revue Sémitique*, 1898, p. 49. Another kind of sin, expiation of which was provided for in the ritual, the *asham* (Levit. v) does not seem to have given rise to a special form of sacrifice. It may be that the sacrifice which expiates it is designated by the name of *asham*, but according to Levit. v, the expiatory ceremony is made up of the *hattat* and the '*olah*; Levit. vii, 2–7, makes the *hattat* and the *asham* identical; cf. Numb. v, 9ff. Yet Ezek. xl, 39; xlii, 13; xlvi, 20, formally distinguish between the two sacrifices.

43. The Marseilles inscription (*C.I.S.* I, 165) likewise reduces the various sacrifices to three types: (1) the *kalil*, which is the equivalent of the Hebrew '*olah*; (2) the *sauat, sacrificium laudis* or *orationis*, equivalent to the *shelamim*; (3) the *shelem-kalil*. Line 11 mentions only two special sacrifices, the *shasaf* and the *hazut* (see

Notes

C.I.S., I, p. 233). Must the *shelem-kalil* be considered as a juxta-position of sacrifices? See G. A. Barton, 'On the Sacrifices Kalil and Shelem-Kalil in the Marseilles Inscription', *Proceedings of the American Oriental Society*, 1894, pp. lxvii–lxix. Inscription 167 (Carthage) distinguishes only *kelilim* and *sauat*. Cf. Clermont-Ganneau, *ibid.*, pp. 597–9.

44. Exod. xxix; Levit. viii.
45. Levit. xii, 6.
46. Levit. xiv. Cf. Levit. xiv, 7, with Exod. xxix, 20.
47. The Greek sacrifices are easily divided into communion sacrifices and expiatory sacrifices, sacrifices to the gods of the under-world and sacrifices to the heavenly gods: they are so classified in Stengel's excellent manual (*GK*). This classification is exact only in appearance.
48. Levit. iv, 9; vii, 14; ix, 21, etc.
49. Levit. x, 16.
50. Ezek. xliii, 19ff; xlv, 19. Cf. the purification of the leper, Levit. xiv, 7.
51. Exod. xxix, 20.

CHAPTER TWO

52. The principle of the entry into the sacrifice is constant in the ritual. It is remarkably expressed in the sacrifice of the *soma*, in which we have the *prayaniyeshti*, the sacrifice of entry, corre-sponding exactly to the *udayaniyeshti*, the sacrifice of exit. *ShB*, 3, 2, 3, 1; 4, 5, 1, 1. Cf. *AitB*, 4, 5, 1 and 2; also *TB*, 5, 6, 1; 5, 3, 4. Generally simple rites and direct consecration suffice to prepare for the sacrifices. But we see that there are cases where the main sacrifice is preceded by preliminary ones. Thus the *praecidaneae* (Aulus Gellius, IV, 6, 7). The Προθύματα are not of the same nature (Euripides, *Iphigenia at Aulis*, 1310–18, cf. Paton, *Cos*, 38, 17; but other sacrifices corresponded to them: *ibid.*, 38, 12.

53. On the *diksha*, see Bruno-Lindner, *Die Diksa oder Weihe für das Somaopfer* (Leipzig, 1878). He studies only the theological texts and compares them. Moreover, these texts of the *ShB*, *AitB*, and *TS* are really complete on this question. H. Oldenberg, *RelV*, pp. 398ff, sees in the *diksha* an ascetic rite comparable to those of shamanism. He attaches no value to the symbolism of the cere-monies and believes it to be of recent date. Oldenberg seems really to have spotlighted one side of the facts; but his explanation is very easily reconcilable with our own. For the whole of the Brahmanic

texts, see S. Lévi, *Sacrifice*, pp. 103–6. For the translation of the word *diksha* we associate ourselves with the opinion of M. Weber (*op. cit.*, n. 32 above, p. 778). The *diksha* is indicated only vaguely in *RV* and had no need to be so. It has a preponderant place in all the rest of the Vedic literature. The success of this rite, which moreover has been very well preserved, was very great in the Puranic and Tantric rituals.

54. See Lévi, *Sacrifice*, p. 103.

55. *TS*, 6, 1, 1, 1.

56. The Hindu texts give an excellent interpretation of this rite, which is found in most religions; the hair, the eyebrows, the beard, the finger- and toe-nails are the 'dead part', the impure part of the body. They are cut in order to make oneself pure. *TS*, 6, 1, 1, 2.

57. Lévi, *Sacrifice*, pp. 87, 88. *TS*, 6, 1, 1, 5. *ShB*, 3, 1, 2, 4 and 5.

58. This is the rite of the *apsudiksha* (*ApShS*, X, 6, 15ff) which symbolizes both his purification (see the mantra *TS*, 1, 2, 1, 1 = *VS* 4, 2, a = *RV*, 10, 17, 10 and *AV* 6, 51, 2) and his new conception. Here is the series of symbols, following *AitB*, 1, 3, 1ff: 'The bath signifies his conception, the hut is the womb, the garment the amnion, the skin of the black antelope the chorion', etc. The schools vary slightly as to the various meanings of the different rites and their order.

59. *ApShS*, X, 6, 6. The mantra is *TB*, 3, 7, 7, 1. Cf. *VS*, 4, 2 and *ShB*, 3, 1, 2, 20.

60. *ApShS*, X, 6, 11ff; X, 7, 1ff; *TS*, 6, 1, 1, 4 and 5, etc.

61. *ApShS*, X, 8, 11 and 12. This antelope skin, according to certain texts (*AitB*, l.c., and *ShB*, 3, 2, 1, 2,) is one of the membranes of the embryo god called the *didikshamana*, the one who initiates. Other texts equally reliable (*TS*, 6, 1, 3, 2,) say that the sacrifier must simply be clad in the skin of a Brahmanic animal, in order to enable him to acquire the quality of a Brahman.

62. *ApShS*, X, 11, 2.

63. *ApShS*, X, 9, 10. *TS*, 6, 1, 3, 3. Cf. Weber, *Indische Studien*, X, p. 358, n. 4.

64. *ApShS*, X, 11, 5ff. *TS*, 6, 1, 4, 3.

65. *ApShS*, X, 11, 7ff; X, 12, 1, 13–18.

66. His *atman*, his individuality. He has become an 'offering to the gods'. *AitB*, 6, 3, 9; 6, 9, 6. *ShB*, 3, 3, 4, 21. *ApShS*, X, 14, 10. 'This is what is explained in the Brahmana. When this *dikshita* becomes lean, he becomes pure (*medhyo*, sacrificial). When there is nothing more, he becomes pure. When his skin touches his bones, he becomes pure. When he is fat he is initiated, when he is lean

he sacrifices. What is missing from his limbs has been sacrificed.'
By fasting the sacrifier has stripped off his mortal body as far as
possible, to put on an immortal form. We see how ascetic practices
took their place in the Hindu system of sacrifice. (See Lévi, *Sacrifice*, p. 83, n. 1. Cf. p. 54.) Developed from this time onwards, they
were able to become, in classical Brahminism, in Jainism, in
Buddhism, the whole of sacrifice. For example, the Buddhist fast
uposatha corresponds exactly to the fast of *upavasatha*, of the
upavasatha night of the ordinary sacrifice, which corresponds to the
fast of *dikshita*. (See *ShB*, 1, 1, 1, 7.) The comparison is made by
Eggeling, *ad loc.* (Sacred Books of the East, XII; cf. *ibid.*, 2, 1, 4, 2,
etc., on the fast of the *diksha*, *ibid.*, 3, 2, 2, 10 and 19.) From the
ShB onwards the virtues of asceticism are considered as great as
those of sacrifice (*ibid.*, 9, 5, 1, 1–7, etc.). We need not point out
the analogy here with Semitic, Greek and Christian practices. The
sacrificial fast of Kippur has become the model for the other Jewish
fasts. These preparatory actions often become the type for the
sacrifice of oneself. The asceticism preliminary to the sacrifice
became, in many cases, the whole sacrifice.

67. A. Hillebrandt, *NVO*, pp. 3, 4. Cf. *ShB*, 1, 1, 1, 7ff, and the
passages cited in the preceding note. Cf. Schwab, *Thieropfer*, p.
xxii, 39.

68. *ShB*, 1, 1, 1, 1ff.

69. Numb. ix, 14; xv, 13–15, 29. Cf. Pausanias, II, 27, 1;
Euripides, *Electra*, 795; *C.I.A.* II, 582, 583.

70. The uncircumcised cannot appear at the cult ceremonies.
Ezek. xliv. 7. Cf. Exod. xii, 43, 45, 48; Levit. xxii, 10, 12, 13.
Herodotus VI, 6. W. Dittenberger, *Sylloge Inscriptionum Graeca-
rum*, 358, cf. 373, 26. In classical and even Vedic India, only the
members of the three higher castes have the right to sacrifice.

71. Athenaeus, IV, 149c; VI, 262c.

72. Dittenberger (see n. 70 above), 373, 9. Festus 82. Lampridius, *Elagabalus*, 6. Cato, *De Agricultura*, lxxxiii, in the sacrifice to Mars Silvanus. The cases of the expulsion of women from
the ceremonies are very numerous.

73. Levit. vii, 19–21; II Chron. xxx, 17, concerning the sacrifice of the Passover. Cf. *C.I.G.* 3562. Yet certain impurities did not
rule out certain sacrifices; e.g., Numb. ix, 10. Cf. *Odyssey* XV, 222ff.

74. Exod. xix. 22.

75. Exod. xix, 10ff; Numb. xi, 18–25. The prohibition of sexual
relations on the occasion of any ceremony is, moreover, an almost
invariable religious principle.

76. Cf. Pausanias X, 32, 9: panegyric of Tithorea.
77. Gen. xxxv, 2; Exod. xix, 14; xl, 12; Levit. viii, 6; Numb.
viii, 7. Stengel, *op. cit.* (n. 22 above), p. 97. J. Marquardt, *Handbuch der Römischen Alterthumer*, VI, p. 248, n. 7. *Iliad*, I, 313ff.
78. Levit. xxiii, 27, 32; the fast of Kippur. Numb. xxix, 7. Cf.
the fast of communicant and priest before the Catholic Mass.
79. See certain examples in Frazer, *GB*, II, 76.
80. Gen. xxxv, 2; Exod. xxix, 8; xl, 13; Levit. viii, 13 (consecration of Aaron). Cf. Pausanias II, 35, 4, procession of the
Chthonia of Hermione. Plutarch, *Consolatio ad Apollonium*, 33
(119). The use of special garments, the daubing of the body or the
face, form part of the ritual of almost all known festivals.
81. Porphyry. See *Vita Pythagorae*, 17.
82. S. Reinach, *Le Voile de l'Oblation* (1897), pp. 5ff.
83. Stengel, *GK*, p. 98. Menander, *The Peasant*, verse 8 (see H.
Weil, 'Le "Campagnard" de Ménandre', *Revue des études grecques*,
1898, p. 123). E. Samter, 'Römische Sühnriten', *Philologus*, 1897,
pp. 394ff. Festus, p. 117.
84. Numb. viii, 7. Lucian, *De dea syria*, 55.
85. For the corpus of ceremonies preparatory (*ihram*=sanctification) to the ancient sacrifices corresponding to the present-day
pilgrimages to Mecca, see J. Wellhausen, *Reste Arabischen Heidentums*, pp. 79 ff. The same practices at the pilgrimages to Hierapolis
(Lucian, *De dea syria*, 55). Likewise for the pilgrims to the ancient
Temple, Jer. xli, 5. See Smith, *RS*, pp. 333, 481 (additional note).
86. The cases that are not borrowed from the domestic ritual and
in which the sacrifier himself officiates are fairly rare in the religions we are studying. In Judaea it was only at the Passover
sacrifice that one could, in the absence of any Levite or Cohen and
outside Jerusalem, slay a victim. In Greece, for example, the sacrifice to Amphiaraos (Oropus) could be presented by the sacrifier in
the absence of a priest (*C.I.G.G.S.*, 235). In the Hindu ritual no
one, unless he is a Brahmin, can sacrifice on the three fires of the
great sacrifice. On the other hand, in the domestic cult, the
presence of a Brahmin was not insisted on. (Hillebrandt, *Ritual
Litteratur* (see n. 10 above), p. 20.)
87. Exod. xxix; Levit. viii; Numb. viii.
88. Ezek. xliv, 9, 11.
89. II Chron. xxx, 17. The Levites sacrifice the Passover for the
impure. In the absence of the Hindu sacrifier, one could carry out
certain essential rites on his behalf (Hillebrandt, *NVO*, p. 146,
n. 1).

90. Exod. xxviii, 38. Numb. xviii, 1, 2, 3.
91. These two characteristics are very noticeable in the Brahmin. On the one hand he is the delegate of the sacrifier, so much so that he becomes the master of his life. (See Lévi, *Sacrifice*, p. 12.) On the other hand he is the delegate of the gods, so much so that he is often treated as one when he is invited to the sacrifice, or when he receives his sacerdotal portion (see below, p. 43, n. 289). On the character of the Brahmin in the ritual, see Weber, *Indische Studien*, X, p. 135. Cf. *ShB*, 1, 7, 1, 5, where the Brahmins are called human gods.
92. Cult of Attis and Cybele, see Frazer, *GB*, p. 300. Pausanias, VIII, 13, 1. Cf. Frazer, *Pausanias*, IV, p. 223; V, p. 261. F. Back, *De Graecorum caerimoniis in quibus homines deorum vice fungebantur* (Berlin, 1883).
93. Pausanias, VI, 20, 1.
94. Pausanias, VIII, 15, 3 (cult of Demeter at Pheneus in Arcadia). Polyaenus, VIII, 59 (cult of Athene at Pellene). See E. Samter, 'Römische Sühnriten, die Trabea' (*Philologus*, LVI, 1897, p. 394) for the garb of the Roman priest. Yet, according to Macrobius, III, 6, 17, the sacrifice at the Ara maxima is carried out with the head veiled, '*ne quis in aede dei habitum ejus imitetur*'.
95. Cf. Frazer, *GB*, I, pp. 286, 288, 343, 368, 370; II, 2, 27; M. Höfler, 'Zur Opfer-Anatomie', *Correspondenzblatt der deutschen Gesellschaft für Anthropologie*, Jhg. XXVII (Jan., 1896, no. 1), 5.
96. In the case in which the Brahmin was himself the sacrifier, and in the case of a *sattra*, a ritual ceremonial and great sacrifice in which the priests were subjected to the *diksha* at the same time as the sacrifier, the king or the great man. In all other cases, only minor lustrations are laid down for the Brahmin: rinsing out the mouth, washing the hands, etc. This rite was always obligatory when evil powers had been mentioned. (*Shankhayana-grihya-sutra*, I, 10, 9; *KShS*, I, 10, 14.
97. Exod. xxx, 20, 21. Cf. Rawlinson, *WAI*, 23, 1, 15, for the hands. The washing of the hands of faithful and priest is customary in the synagogue as well as in Catholic ritual.
98. Levit. x, 9; Ezek. xliv, 21; Josephus, *Antiquities*, 3, 12, 2; Josephus, *De Bello Judaico*, 5, 5, 7; Philo, *De Ebrietate*, 127ff.
99. Levit. vi, 10; xvi, 4, 32. Cf. Exod. xxviii, 40, 42.
100. Levit. xvi, 4; xvi, 23. Ezek. xliv, 19.
101. Exod. xxviii, 35; Ezek. xlii, 11–14 (the Septuagint text is to be preferred).
102. Exod. xxviii, 43; xxx, 20, 21.

103. Levit. x, 1ff.

104. I Sam. iv, 11.

105. See the legendary story in Talmud Jerus., *Yoma*, Gemara, I, 1, 5 (tr. Schwab), which says that a high priest who committed a ritual heresy on Yom Kippur would die on the spot, that worms would come out of his nose, and the shoe from a calf's hoof from his forehead, as had happened to the priests of the family of Baithos.

106. Cf. *Tosefta Sukkah*, III, 16.

107. We use the Mishnah and Talmud of Jerusalem, referring the reader for convenience to Schwab's French translation: *Yoma*, chs. II, III, Schwab V, p. 155. See on this subject: J. Derenbourg, 'Essai de restitution de l'ancienne rédaction de Massechet Kippourim', *Revue d'études juives*, VI (1882), 41ff; M. T. Houtsma, 'Over de israëlietische Vastendagen', *Verslagen en Mededeelingen der koninklijke Akad. v. Wetensch.*, *Afdeel. Letterk.*, Amsterdam, 1897–8, vol. XII, part II, pp. 3ff.

108. Levit. xvi.

109. Levit. xvi, 2.

110. Talm. Jerus., *Yoma* (Schwab trans., p. 161). On the occasion of Kippur sacerdotal purity was reinforced, and absolute isolation was attained.

111. During these seven days the high priest conducts the service in full pontifical robes, which, as we know, had special virtues (Exod. xxviii).

112. The cell of Beth-Abdinos.

113. *Yoma*, Mishnah, I, 5. The Gemara (*ad loc.*) gives several explanations of this rite, which has not been understood. One of them seems to indicate what may have been the true meaning: the old men weep because they are forced to abandon, thus isolated, the pontiff whose life is at the same time so precious and so fragile.

114. For this vigil he either carries on biblical exegesis himself, or listens to the learned men, or passages from the Bible are read to him. The direction that he occupy himself during the night before the sacrifice with the sacred writings, that he speak of them and them alone, is also a directive in Hindu sacrifice; it is also a directive for the Sabbath and for feast-days generally, in the majority of known rituals. The Christian vigils, at first especially for Easter, later increased in number, were perhaps an imitation of the learned discourses on the eve of the Jewish Passover.

115. Seminal losses—that is the explanation, a correct but incomplete one, given in our text. In fact, it must be remembered that sleep is very usually considered a dangerous state; for the soul

is then in movement, outside the body, to which it may not be able to return. Now the death of the high priest would be a calamity. This is forestalled by requiring him to keep vigil. Sleep is likewise a dangerous state for the Hindu *dikshita*, who sleeps under the protection of Agni, by the fire, in a special position (cf. *TS*, 6, 1, 4, 5 and 6).

116. Talmud, *Yoma*, I, 2, and Gemara, p. 168; cf. Mishnah, *ibid.*, III, 3.

117. Hemerology of the month of Elul. *WAI*, I, IV, p. 32, 3. See Jastrow, *The Original Character of the Hebrew Sabbath.*

118. Stengel, *GK*, p. 13 (sacrifices to the heavenly gods).

119. Stengel, *GK* (sacrifices to the Chthonian gods). Pausanias, II, 24, 1 (Argos), sacrifice to Apollo Δειραδιώτης. See p. 54 below for the sacrifice of the bull to Rudra. The fixing of the day and hour at which the sacrifice must be made is one of the most carefully detailed points in Hindu and other rituals. The constellation under which the sacrifice takes place is also not a matter of indifference.

120. Levit. xvii, 3–5.

121. It must be understood that we do not wish to lay down any priority in time for the place permanently consecrated over the place consecrated for a set occasion. We reserve judgement completely on this question.

122. Exod. xxix, 37, 44; Numb. ix, 15ff; II Sam. vi, 17; I Kings viii, 63, etc. As regards the prohibition against sacrificing elsewhere than in Jerusalem, see Levit. xvii, 3–4; Deut. xii, 5ff; xiv, 23; xv, 20; xvi, 2ff. It is certain that this prohibition dates from later times. See II Kings xxiii. It even seems that 'lesser altars' always existed in Palestine. Talm. Babyl., Mishnah *Megillah*, 9b; cf. Talm. Babyl., *Zebahim*, 116a.

123. Exod. xx, 24; Deut. xii, 5, etc.

124. Exod. xxix, 42–6, etc.

125. Exod. xxix, 38. Cf. Porphyry, *De abstinentia*, I, 25, etc. Concerning the perpetuity of the altar fire, and the way in which Israel's destiny is linked up with that of the Temple, see especially Dan. ix, 27; viii, 11–15; xi, 31, etc. This became a legendary theme in Jewish literature.

126. Exod. xxx, 10; Ezek. xlvi, 14.

127. Provided that it was propitious and declared 'sacrificial' by the Brahmins.

128. On the setting up of the fires, see Hillebrandt (*Ritual Litteratur*, see n. 10 above), sect. 59. Koulikovski, 'Les Trois Feux.

sacrés du Rig-Veda' (*Revue de l'histoire des religions*, XX (1889), pp. 151ff), deals only with the division of the fires. Weber, *Indische Studien*, IX, p. 216. Eggeling on *ShB* (Sacred Books of the East, XII, pp. 247ff).

129. The materials with and on which it is lighted and prepared (the Sambharas) all correspond to a very important myth (*TB*, 1, 1, 3 and 5; cf. *ShB*, 2, 1, 4). They are things in which something igneous, particularly animate, seems to dwell: so animate themselves that legend sees in certain of them the primitive forms of the world. This creation of fire symbolizes the creation of the world.

130. The fire is always created by friction at the time of the placing of the fires, of an animal sacrifice, of the sacrifice of the soma. See Schwab, *Thieropfer*, sect. 47, pp. 77ff. Weber, *Indische Studien*, I, 197, n. 3. A Kuhn, *Herabkunft des Feuers und des Göttertranks* (Gütersloh, 1886), pp. 70ff. Around this creation of the fire-god the Brahmins wove, from the *RV* onwards, pantheistic conceptions. For the fire of sacrifice alone is excelling, it alone is the complete Agni, containing the 'three bodies of Agni'—his terrestrial essence (the domestic fire), his atmospheric essence (the lightning), and his heavenly essence (the sun); it contains all that is animate, warm, and 'igneous' in the world (*TB*, 1, 2, 1, 3 and 4).

131. It is even one of the oldest epithets of Agni. See A. Bergaigne, *La Religion Védique* (Paris, 1878–83), II, p. 217.

132. See note 130 above.

133. Levit. x, 2; Judges vi, 11ff, the sacrifice of Gideon; xiii, 19ff, Manoah; I Kings xviii, 38, Elijah; I Chron. xxi, 26, etc. The preparation of the fires bulks large in other rituals. On the necessity of a pure fire, cf. Levit. x, 1; on the renewing of the fires in Mexico: Sahagun, *Historia de las cosas de Nueva España*, II, p. 18; Chavero, *Mexico a través de los siglos*, I, p. 77; at Lemnos: Philostratus, *Heroikos*, XIX, 14; L. Couve, 'Inscription de Delphes', *Bulletin de correspondance hellénique*, XVIII (1894), pp. 87 and 92; in Ireland, A. Bertrand, *Religion des Gaulois* (Paris, 1897), p. 106. Cf. Frazer, *GB*, II, pp. 76, 194. Frazer, *Pausanias*, II, p. 392; V, p. 521. For Indo-European religions see Knauer in *Festgrüss for Roth*, p. 64.

134. It becomes the '*devayajana*', the place of sacrifice to the gods. One must refer to the mystical speculations of the Brahmins on this point. The '*devayajana*' is the only solid ground on earth. The earth itself exists only to serve as the place of sacrifice to the gods. This special site is also the base of operations of the gods, their citadel; it is from there that, taking off in a bound (devayatana)

they ascended into heaven. It is moreover the centre of heaven and earth, the navel of the earth. However foolish such expressions appear, we must recall that for the Jews the temple was the centre of the earth, just as Rome was for the Romans; and on medieval maps Jerusalem was the navel of the world. These ideas are not so outlandish. The religious centre of life coincides with the centre of the world.

135. The name has even become that of the Buddhist monasteries. We cannot follow either the detail or the order of the rites in the Hindu animal sacrifice. Thus the ceremony of the lighting of the fire is declared by at least one school (*KShS*, VI, 3, 26) to be inseparable from the ceremonies of bringing in the victim.

136. See the ground plans in Hillebrandt, *NVO*, p. 191, and Eggeling, Sacred Books of the East, XXVI, 475.

137. It is exactly measured out and takes on the most varied shapes according to the sacrifice. (See Hillebrandt, *NVO*, pp. 47ff, 176ff; Schwab, *Thieropfer*, pp. 13ff; Thibaut, 'Baudhayana Shulba-paribhasha sutra', in *Pandit*, Benares, IX (1875).) In the case of our animal sacrifice there are two *vedi*, one of which is approximately the ordinary *vedi* that we describe in the text, the other which is *raised up* (see Schwab, pp. 14, 21), on which there is a fire which is one of the sacrificial fires (*ApShS*, VII, 7, 3; see Schwab, p. 37). Due allowance being made, they are built up or hollowed out in the same way.

138. *TS*, 1, 1, 9, 1, 9. The mantras express the fact that the evil omens have been repelled, that the gods are protecting the *vedi* on all sides. Those which accompany the building up of the *uttara vedi* rather express the second idea (*TS*, 1, 2, 12, 2), especially those which accompany the lustration of the altar which has been constructed.

139. From the *RV* onwards the gods bear the epithet '*barhish-adas*', those who are sitting on the site of the sacrifice. (See H. G. Grassmann, *Wörterbuch zum Rig-Veda* (Leipzig, 1873), *ad verbum*.) Cf. *RV*, II, 3, 4; V, 31, 12; VI, 1, 10, etc.

140. See Schwab, *Thieropfer*, pp. 11, 47. Ordinarily the sacred utensils of a temple may not be removed from it. Thus at Jerusalem the knives were shut away in a special cell, that of the *halifoth*. (See Talmud Jerus., *Sukkah*, Gemara, V, 8 (Schwab trans., VI, p. 51); *Middoth*, Gemara, IV, 7; *Yoma*, III, 8.) Special sacrifices, such as the domestic sacrifice of the Passover, demand a brand-new vessel; likewise in Greece, see Paton, *Cos*, 38, 25; 39, 6. Cf. Frazer, *GB*, II, p. 107.

141. Sèe Schwab, *Thieropfer*, p. 44, for the enumeration of these instruments. *ApShS*, VII, 8. For the purification see Schwab, no. 35.

142. *ApShS*, VII, 9, 6. It is planted in such a way that one half is within the bounds of the *vedi*, the other half outside it.

143. They search for the tree with the specified quality (*TS*, 6, 3, 3, 4; *ApShS*, VII, 1, 16 and 17. See Schwab, *Thieropfer*, pp. 2ff.) It is worshipped and propitiated (*ApShS*, VII, 2, 1); it is anointed; it is felled with caution; the stump is anointed and an incantation uttered. All these ceremonies clearly indicate, as Oldenberg perceived, an ancient vegetation cult (*RelV.*, p. 256). Oldenberg (p. 90) compares this stake to sacrificial stakes in general, and particularly to the Semitic *asherah*, also planted on the altar. (See Smith, *RS*, p. 187, n. 1.) The two comparisons are in part justified.

144. *ApShS*, VII, 10, 1ff. For the meaning of the rite, *TS*, 6, 3, 4, 2 and 3. The whole rite is certainly ancient. While the *yupa* is being anointed, and while it is being dug in and placed upright, mantras of the *RV* are recited (the *hotar*; *ApShS*, 3, 1, 8). The mantras are in the following order: I, 36, 13–14; III, 8, 13, 2.5.4 (the *apri* hymn); in the case when several animals are sacrificed and several stakes erected, III, 8, 6, 11. The same ritual is prescribed *AitB*, 6, 2, 17, 23, which comments on the verses of the *RV*. This hymn already expresses the different functions of the *yupa*, which slays demons, protects mankind, symbolizes life, bears up the offering to the gods, supports heaven and earth. Cf. *TS*, 6, 3, 4, 1 and 3.

145. The sacrifier also remains for a certain time holding the *yupa*. (*ApShS*, 7, 11, 5. According to certain sutras, the woman and the officiant also remain there. The tradition of the Apastambins seems preferable.) In any case it is the sacrifier who carries out part of the anointing, and passes his hand along the whole length of the stake. All these rites have as their object the identification of the sacrifier with the stake and with the victim, whose place he is made for a time to take.

146. *AitB*, 6, 1, 1; cf. *ShB*, 1, 6, 2, 1, etc.

147. *TS*, 6, 3, 4, 3 and 4. Cf. *TS*, 6, 3, 4, 7; *ShB*, 3, 7, 1, 2, 5.

148. It has the height of the sacrifier when the latter is in a chariot, or standing with upraised arms (*TS*, 6, 3, 4, 1; *ApShS*, VII, 2, 11ff.)

149. *TS*, 6, 3, 4, 4.

150. We assume that what is valid for the *vedi* and the *yupa* is also generally so for the altars, baetyls (sacred stones) and raised

stones on which or at the foot of which the sacrifice is made. The altar is the symbol of the covenant between man and the gods. Throughout the sacrifice the profane is being united to the divine.

151. Hence the prayer uttered at the beginning of any sacrifice by the sacrifier, 'May I measure up to this rite' (*ShB*, 1, 1, 1, 7). Hence especially the metaphor, common in the Sanskrit texts, which compares the sacrifice to a cloth which is being woven and hung. *RV*, X, 130; Bergaigne and Henry, *Manuel pour étudier le sanscrit védique*, p. 125n.; Lévi, *Sacrifice*, p. 79, p. 80, n. 1.

152. See Lévi, *Sacrifice*, pp. 23ff. Any ritual error is a *cut* made in the cloth of sacrifice. By this act the magic forces escape and cause the sacrifier to die, or go mad, or be ruined. We have no need to recall the famous cases related in the Bible of ritual heresies terribly punished; the sons of Eli, the leprosy of king Uzziah, etc. This is because it is perilous, as a general rule, to handle sacred things; for example, in Vedic India one must take care that the sacrifier does not touch the *vedi* (*ShB*, 1, 2, 5, 4), touches no one with the magical wooden sword, etc.

153. The ritual expiations have it in fact as their aim to isolate the effects of the errors committed in the course of the rite (see above). Cf. Servius on *Aeneid*, IV, 696: *et sciendum si quid caerimoniis non fuerit observatum, piaculum admitti*. Arnobius, IV, 31. Cicero, *De haruspicum responso*, XI, 23. In the same way the frontal of the high priest at Jerusalem expiated any slight errors committed during the rite: Exod. xxviii, 38. Cf. Talmud Jerus., *Yoma*, II, 1 (trans. Schwab, V, p. 176).

154. Here we have a curious parallel with the theories of the Jewish ritual. A lamb consecrated for the Passover sacrifice could not be changed (Talmud, *Pesachim*, Mishnah, IX, 6). In the same way a beast set apart for a sacrifice must be sacrificed, even if the sacrifier dies (*ibid.*, *Hagigah*, Gemara, I, 1, *ad fin.*; Schwab, VI, p. 261). For the same reason, on the eve of Kippur all the animals that were to be slaughtered on the following day were paraded before the high priest, so that he did not confuse the various victims.

155. As we know, the attitude usually recommended is one of silence. See below, p. 33. Cf. Marquardt, *op. cit.* (n. 77 above), VI, p. 178.

156. See Lévi, *Sacrifice*, pp. 112ff.

157. These cases include those in which the victims are, or have been, totemic creatures. But it is not logically necessary that sacred animals, for example, should always have this character (see

Marillier, *Revue de l'histoire des religions*, XXXVII (1898), pp.
230ff; Frazer, *GB*, II, pp. 135-8), as, for example, is maintained by
Jevons (*Introduction to the History of Religion*, London, 1896,
p. 55). This theory is in part upheld by Robertson Smith, *Kinship*
(see n. 5 above), pp. 308ff, and *RS*, pp. 357ff. The truth is that in
one way or another there is a definite relation between the god
and his victim, and the latter often arrives at the sacrifice already
consecrated; cf. Stengel, *GK*, pp. 107ff; Marquardt (n. 77 above),
p. 172; P. Foucart, 'Inscriptions de l'Acropole', *Bulletin de correspondance hellénique*, XIII (1889), p. 169; Scholion on Apollonius
Rhodius, II, 549 (sacrifice of doves); W. M. Ramsay, *Cities and
Bishoprics of Phrygia*, I, p. 138; Pausanias, III, 14, 9, and Frazer
ad loc.; Plutarch, *Quaestiones Romanae*, 111; Athenaeus, VIII,
346d (sacrifice of fish at Hierapolis), etc. In other cases, the god
refused certain victims. E.g., Pausanias, X, 32, 8; Herodotus, IV,
63; Pausanias, II, 10, 4. Yahweh never allowed any but the four
kinds of pure animals: sheep, cattle, goats, and doves.

158. This again is a very general case; thus the horse of the
ashvamedha was tended and worshipped for many months. (See A.
Hillebrandt, 'Nationale Opfer in Alt-Indien', in *Festgruss to
Böhtlingk* (Stuttgart, 1888), pp. 40ff; in the same way were treated
the *meriah* of the Khonds, the bear of the Ainu, etc., all well-
known cases.

159. This is a Vedic prescription, as well as a Biblical and perhaps
a general one. For the Hindu animal sacrifice, see Schwab, *Thieropfer*, p. xviii; H. Zimmer, *Altindisches Leben* (Berlin, 1879), p. 131;
KShS, 6, 3, 22 and paddh. *ApShS*, VII, 12, 1 and commentary, *TS*,
5, 1, 1. On the Temple victims, see Exod. xii, 5; Levit. xxii, 19ff;
Deut. xv. 21; xvii, 1; Malachi i, 6-14, etc. Cf. Stengel, *GK*, p. 107.

160. Thus the horse of the *ashvamedha* had to be red (it bore the
name *Rohita*—red—and was a symbol of the sun. See Henry,
Les Hymnes Rohita de l'Atharva-Véda (Paris, 1889). On red
victims, see Festus, 45; Diodorus, I, 88; cf. Frazer, *GB*, II, 59.
On black cows, to bring rain, see below, p. 66. In Greece (Stengel,
GK, p. 134), the victims destined for the heavenly gods were
generally light in colour; those offered to the Chthonian gods were
always black.

161. See below, p. 65.

162. Paton, *Cos*, 37, 22. Stengel, *GK*, pp 97ff. Mannhardt,
WFK, II, p. 108.

163. *Iliad*, X, 294; *Odyssey*, III, 384. Cf. Rawlinson, *WAI*,
IV, pp. 22, 37ff. Cf. below p. 57.

Notes

164. Pausanias, X, 32, 9.
165. Cf. Frazer, *GB*, pp. 145, 198, etc.
166. Chavero, *Mexico a través de los siglos*, p. 644.
167. Porphyry, *De abstinentia*, II, 54.
168. *ApShS*, VII, 12, 1.
169. *ApShS*, VII, 12, 10. The mantras for these libations are *TS*, 1, 4, 2. It is curious that these mantras are to be found also at *AV*, II, 34, cf. Weber, *Indische Studien*, III, p. 207, and they are employed (*KauS*, 57, 20) at the initiation of the young Brahmin. This is because it is a kind of introduction into the religious world. Libations at the presentation of the victim are fairly often found. Paton, *Cos*, 40, 9. In Assyria, Inscription of Sippora, IV, 32.
170. *TS*, 1, 3, 7, 1; 6, 3, 6, 1-2; *ApShS*, VII, 12, 6. Cf. *VS*, 6, 5. *Maitr. S.*, 5, 3, 9, 6. *ShB*, 3, 7, 3, 9ff. *KShS*, 6, 3, 19.
171. *ApShS*, VII, 12, 6. In the present case the god is Prajapati-Rudra. *TS*, 3, 1, 4, 1, commented upon by *TS*, 3, 1, 4, 5. This invocation is not practised by other schools.
172. Marquardt, *op. cit.* (n. 77 above), VI, p. 175. Cf. Frazer, *GB*, II, pp. 110ff. It was even more natural when a human sacrifice was intended (see Servius on *Aeneid*, III, 57. Cf. Euripides, *Heraclidae*, 550ff; *Phoenissae*, 890; Athenaeus, XIII, 602. Chavero (see n. 166 above), p. 610. (Cf. Samuel C. Macpherson, *Memorials of Service in India* (London, 1865), p. 146), and yet more so when a god was the victim.
173. *ApShS*, VII, 13, 8. The mantra is *TS*, 1, 3, 8, 1, commented 6, 3, 6, 3, *dhrisha manusha*, 'Strengthen yourself, O man!' Another tradition, *VS*, VI, 8, *ShB*, 3, 7, 4, 1, has it that the formula to be addressed to the animal is *dhrisha manushan*, 'strengthen men'. We believe, contrary to the opinion of Schwab (*Thieropfer*, p. 81, n. 2) that the text of *TS* is the better founded, according to the nature of the rite. The Vajasaneyins represent, here as elsewhere, a more purified and rationalized tradition. The comparison with *RV*, I, 63, 3, is not convincing.
174. *ApShS*, VII, 13, 9 and commentary. They say to it, 'You are a drinker of water.' (*VS*, VI, 10a. *TS*, 1, 3, 8, 1.) Ludwig on *RV*, X, 36, 8. V, IV, p. 233, thinks (cf. Sayana *ad TS*) that the meaning is 'You are thirsty for water.' But the meaning we adopt is that indicated in *ShB*, 3, 7, 4, 6. Cf. *TS*, 6, 3, 6, 4 *ad fin.*, as well as the commentaries on the *VS*, *loc. cit.*, and on *KShS*, 6, 3, 32. By giving the animal something to drink, it is made internally pure. In the same way the sacrifier rinses out his mouth before sacrifice.
175. *ApShS*, VII, 13, 10.

176. H. von Fritze, 'Οὐλαί', *Hermes*, XXXII (Berlin, 1897), pp. 235ff. Stengel thinks that the οὐλαί are the bread of the divine meal. At Megara, in the sacrifice to Tereus, the οὐλαί are replaced by pebbles. Pausanias I, 41, 9. Cf. E. Lefébure, 'Origines du fétichisme', in *Mélusine* (Paris), 1896–7, col. 151, and F. Sessions, 'Some Syrian Folklore Notes', *Folklore*, 1898, p. 15. In Sicily the companions of Ulysses, when they sacrificed three bullocks to the sun, used leaves as οὐλαί. Cf. Pausanias, II, 9, 4. The casting of οὐλαί can be a means of communication between the sacrifier and the victim, or a fertility lustration comparable to the casting of seeds over the bride.

177. This is the ceremony of *paryagnikriya* or circumambulation with fire. *ApShS*, VII, 15, 1. The rite is certainly of the greatest antiquity, for the priest (the *maitravaruna*, cf. Weber, *Indische Studien*, IX, p. 188) repeats (*AshvShS*, II, 2, 9ff) the hymn *RV*, IV, 5, 1–3 (see Oldenberg's translation and notes in Sacred Books of the East, XLVI, ad loc.) The meaning of the rite is threefold. It is firstly a walking round the fire of Agni, the divine priest of the gods, repository of the treasures, who consecrates the victim, and conducts him towards the gods by showing him the way (such is the meaning of the three verses of the *RV* used on this occasion and composed specially for it), cf. *AitB*, 6.5.1 and 6.11.3. The victim was thereby made divine, cf. *TS*, 6, 3, 8, 2, *ShB*, 3, 8, 1, 6. Secondly it is simply a magic circle. The evil spirits that prowl around the victim like the gods are driven off. Finally it is a beneficent ritual circumambulation, made from left to right, in the direction of the gods (*Baudh. shr. sutra*, II, 2, cited by Caland, *op. cit.* below, p. 287), which has in itself a magic power. On circumambulations of the victim, see W. Simpson, *The Buddhist Praying Wheel* (London, 1896), and especially the exhaustive monograph of Caland, 'Een indo-germaansch Lustratie-Gebruik' (*Verslag en Mededeelingen der koninklijke Akad. voor Wetenschaapen*, Afdeeling Letterkunde, vol. XII, part 2, Amsterdam, 1898, pp. 275ff). In the first place the rite is fundamental in the Hindu ritual, both domestic (cf. *Par. Grihya Sutra*, 1, 1, 2) and solemn (Hillebrandt, *NVO*, p. 42). Cf. *ShB*, 1, 2, 2 and 3. See Caland, *op. cit.*, p. 300, notes 2 and 3; in the second place, almost general among the Indo-European populations (see Caland); finally, it is very widespread almost everywhere.

178. II Kings iii, 27; Ezek. xvi, 36. Cf. Gen. xxii; Deut. xii, 31. Ps. cv (cvi), 37; Isa. lvii, 5. Lucian, *De dea syria*, 58. Cf. the legend of Athamas. Preller, *Griechische Mythologie*, II, p. 312. Cf. R.

Notes

Basset, *Nouveaux Contes Berbères* (Paris, 1897), no. 91. Cf. M.
Höfler (see n. 95 above), 3. Cf. the sacrifice of a member of the
family. Porphyry, *De abstinentia*, II, 27. Cf. the legend of Shunah-
shepa (Lévi, *Sacrifice*, p. 135). The examples of this new representation are specially numerous in the building sacrifice. See
Sartori (n. 27 above), p. 17.
179. See above, p. 10, e.g., I Chron. xxi, 23ff, the story of David
and Ornan's threshing-floor.
180. Levit. i, 4; iii, 2; iv, 4; xvi, 21. Exod. xxix, 15, 19; cf.
Numb. viii, 10; xxvii, 18, 23. Cf. Deut. xxxiv, 9. Ps. lxxxviii
(lxxxix), 26. Tylor, *Primitive Culture*, II, p. 3. Smith, *RS*, p. 423.
181. *ApShS*, VII, 15, 10, 11. The mantra then says, *TS*, 3, 1,
4, 3, that the 'breath', the life of the sacrifier, is, like his desire,
linked with the destiny of the animal, 3, 1, 5, 1. The school of the
White Yajurveda does not lay down any mantra (*KShS*, VI, 5, 5),
and moreover does not cause any expiatory offerings to be made
at this juncture, a notable difference. But the rite of communication, as well as the theory of it, remains the same. *ShB*, 3, 8, 1, 10.
TS, 6, 3, 8, 1. The Brahmins are arguing. 'The animal must be
touched', some of them say; 'But it is being led to its death; if he
(the sacrifier) touched it from behind, the yajamana would die on
the spot.' Others say: 'It is being led to heaven, and if he (the
sacrifier) did not touch it from behind, he would be separated from
heaven. That is why it must be touched with the two skewers of
the vapa. Thus it is as it were touched and not touched.' (Cf. 6,
3, 5, 1.) The *ShB* explains that the communication is a mysterious
one, both harmless and useful for the sacrifier, whose prayer and
soul go with the victim to heaven.
182. We do not study the question of the 'presentation' of the
victim to the god, and the invocation that more often than not
accompanies it. We should be led into overlong explanations, for
in this lie the connexions between sacrifice and prayer. Let us
merely say that there are (1) manual rites, such as tying the animal
to the stake (see above, p. 30), and to the horns of the altar (Ps.
cxvii (cxviii), 27; cf. Smith, *RS*, p. 322; Levit. i, 11); (2) oral
rites: the invitation to the gods; hymns to the gods; a description
of the qualities of the victim; a definition of the results expected.
Consecration is called down from on high by all these means
combined.
183. We allude to the so-called *apavyani* libations of the Hindu
animal sacrifice (Schwab, *Thieropfer*, p. 98, no. 1, a in *TB*, 3, 8,
17, 5, links the word with the root *pu*, to purify). They are to be

Notes

found elsewhere only in the schools of the Black Yajurveda. They are carried out during the act of separation of the animal by means of the circumambulation of the fire, and at the moment when it is being led to the place of slaughter (*ApShS*, VII, 15, 4; the mantras are: *TS*, 3, 1, 4, 1, 2, explained in *TS*, 3, 1, 5,1. They are found again in *MS*, 1, 2, 1). The formulas explain that the gods are taking possession of the animal and that it is going up to heaven; that this animal represents the others, among those beasts whose master is Rudra-Prajapati; that it is acceptable to the gods, and will give life and wealth in the form of cattle; that it is the portion of Rudra-Prajapati who, on recovering his offspring and tying it up, 'is about to cease binding [putting to death] the living, animals or men', etc.

184. Stengel, *GK*, p. 101. Herodotus, ii, 39, 40. At Rome, Marquardt, *op. cit.* n. 77 above, p. 192. Smith, *RS*, pp. 430f. Frazer, *GB*, I, p. 364; II, pp. 102ff. Perhaps with these practices must be compared the mourning of the Flaminica, at the festival of the Argeii: Plutarch, *Quaestiones Romanae*, 86.

185. This rite, very widespread, as Frazer has shown, is expressed in a remarkable fashion in the Hindu ritual. At the moment of the suffocation, among the formulas recited by the officiating priest, the *maitravaruna*—the formulas of the *adhrigunigada* (*AshvShS*, III, 3,1 explained in *AitB*, 6, 6, 1), which are reckoned among the most ancient in the Vedic ritual—is one that reads as follows: 'They have abandoned to us this creature, its mother and father, its sister and its brother of the same stock, and its companion of the same race.' (*ApShS*, VII, 25, 7, with *TS*, 3, 6, 11, 12. See Schwab, *Thieropfer*, p. 141 n., and *ShB*, 3, 8, 3, 11; *ApShS*, VII, 16, 7.—Cf. *TS*, 6, 3, 8, 3, and *ShB*, 3, 8, 1, 15.)

186. The *shamitar*, the 'appeaser', the euphemistic name for the sacrificer, may or may not be a Brahmin (*ApShS*, VII, 17, 14). In any case, he is a Brahmin of lower rank, for he bears the sin of having killed a sacred, sometimes an inviolable, creature. In the ritual is to be found a kind of imprecation against him: 'Among your whole race, may such an appeaser never do such things', that is to say, 'May you have no sacrificer among your relatives.' (We follow the text of the *AshvShS*, III, 3, 1, which Schwab also follows, *Thieropfer*, p. 105, and not the text of *AitB*, 6, 7, 11.)

187. Aelian, *De Natura animalium*, XII, 34 (Tenedos). Smith, *RS*, p. 305.

188. Porphyry, *De abstinentia*, II, 29–30; Pausanias, I, 24, 4; 28, 10. Myth of the institution of the Karneia: Pausanias, III,

Notes

13, 4; Usener, 'Göttliche Synonyme', *Rheinisches Museum*, 1898, pp. 359ff. Stengel, *GK*, p. 140. Plato, *Laws*, IX, 865.

189. See Frazer, *Pausanias*, III, pp. 54ff.

190. They say: 'Turn his feet to the north, let his eye face the sun, scatter his breath to the winds, his life to the atmosphere, to the regions his hearing, to the earth his body.' These directions in *AshvShS*, III, 3, 1; cf. *AitB*, 6, 6, 13, are important. The head is turned towards the west, because that is the general path of things; the one that the sun takes, that the dead follow, that by which the gods ascended into heaven, etc. The orientation of the victim is a very noteworthy fact. Unfortunately the information, whether Semitic, classical or ethnographical, that we possess on the question is relatively sparse. In Judaea the victims were tied to the horns of the altar, on different sides according to the nature of the sacrifice, and seem to have had their heads turned towards the east. In Greece, the victims offered to the Chthonian gods were sacrificed head downwards; those sacrificed to the heavenly gods had their heads pointed towards the sky. (See *Iliad*, I, 459 and scholium.) Cf. the bas-reliefs representing the Mithraic sacrifice of the bull, in F. Cumont, *Textes et monuments relatifs aux mystères de Mithra*.

191. *ApShS*, VII, 17. 1. *AshvShS*, III, 3, 6. In the same way, Catholic worshippers bow their heads at the Elevation in the Mass.

192. The animal is told that it is going up to heaven for the sake of its own kind, that it is not to die, that it is not being harmed, that it is going the way of the good, on the path of Savitar (the sun), the road of the gods, etc. *ApShS*, VII, 16. *TB*, 3, 7, 7, 14.

193. *KShS* VI, 15, 19. It is important that the body be still intact at the moment of death.

194. Such is the order that is repeated three times. *AshvShS*, III, 3, 1, 4.

195. E.g., in G. Maspero, 'Sur un décret d'excommunication trouvé au Djebel-Barkal', *Revue archéologique*, 1871, NS vol. 22, pp. 335ff (the Napata stele).

196. This took place in all cases in the Hebrew ritual (Levit. i, 4, etc.) save at the sacrifice of the doves, where the throat was opened with the finger-nail (Levit. i, 14, 15). In Greece, see *Odyssey*, III, 449. Apollonius Rhodius, *Argonautica*, I, 429ff. Sophocles, *Ajax*, 296ff.

197. The stoning of Pharmakos at the Thargelia: Euripides, *Andromache*, 1128; Istros, *Fragmenta Histor. Graec.*, I, p. 422. Cf. the festival of the λιθοβόλια at Troezen, Pausanias, II, 32.

Cf. Mannhardt, *WFK*, I, 419, 548, 552. The stoning seems to
have been to 'divide the responsibility' among the bystanders.
Jevons, *Introduction to the History of Religion*, p. 292. For the
victim struck from a distance, see Suidas, Βουτύπος. Cf. Porphyry,
De abstinentia, II, 54ff.
198. Dionysius of Halicarnassus, VII, 72, 15. Apollonius Rhodius, *Argonautica*, I, 426. *Odyssey*, XIV, 425.
199. Smith, *RS*, p. 370.
200. In Vedic India a series of expiations was laid down for the
case where the animal, at his entry into the field of sacrifice, made
sinister signs. (*TB*, 3, 7, 8, 1 and 2; see commentary. See Schwab,
Thieropfer, p. 76, no. 46); likewise for the case where the animal
uttered a cry after being prepared for suffocation, or touched its
belly with its hoof. *ApShS*, VII, 17, 2, 3. Cf. *TS*, 3, 1, 5, 2. For other
data see Weber, *Omina et Portenta*, pp. 377ff.
201. We recall the Biblical principle whereby all blood shed was
consecrated to God, even that of animals killed in the chase; Levit.
iii, 17; xvii, 10; Deut. xii, 16, 23; xv, 23. Cf. in Greece, *Odyssey*,
III, 455; XIV, 427. Stengel, *GK*, p. 401. Höfler, *op. cit.* n. 95
above, p. 5. The same precaution was taken with regard to milk;
Höfler, *op. cit.*, *ibid.*
202. In Judaea the blood was caught in vessels and handed over
to the officiating priest, Levit. i, 5; ix, 12, and he used it in ritual.
In Greece, in some sacrifices, the blood was caught in a goblet,
σφάγιον or σφαγεῖον. Pollux, X, 65. Xenophon, *Anabasis*, II, 2, 9.
203. Smith, *RS*, p. 417. Scythian sacrifice, Herodotus, IV, 60;
among certain tribes of the Altai the victim's backbone was
broken. N. Kondakof *et al.*, *Antiquités de la Russie méridionale*
(Paris, 1891), p. 181.
204. Pausanias, VIII, 37, 8. Smith, *RS*, p. 368.
205. Mannhardt, *WFK*, I, pp. 28ff.
206. Plutarch, *De Iside et Osiride*, 15, 17; Mannhardt, *WFK*,
II, 52; Rohde, *Psyche* (Engl. trans.), p. 302. A. Dieterich, *Nekyia*
(Leipzig, 1893), pp. 197ff, etc.
207. Wiedemann, *Aeg. Zeitschr.*, 1878, p. 89. Cf. Morgan,
J. J. M. de, *Recherches sur les origines de l'Égypte: Ethnographie
préhistorique et tombeau royal de Négadah* (Paris, 1897), p. 215.
Cf. Frazer, *GB*, II, p. 90.
208. Herodotus, III, 91. See the known facts in Frazer, *GB*,
II, pp. 112ff.
209. Levit. iv, 5, 7; 16–19; xvii, 11. This last passage is often
relied upon to prove that the expiatory force of the sacrifice belongs

to the blood. But this text simply means that the blood placed on the altar represents the life of the consecrated victim.

210. Exod. xxx, 10; Levit. xvi, 16. See especially Talmud Jerus., *Yoma*, Mishnah, V, 4, 6.

211. Levit. iv, 25, 30; viii, 15; ix, 9; xvi, 15; Ezek. xliii, 20.

212. Levit. i, 5; ix, 12. Levit: iii, 12.

213. The custom of painting certain idols red doubtless arose from these primitive forms of anointing. See Frazer, *Pausanias*, III, pp. 2off. Herodotus, IV, 62. A. Sprenger, *Das Leben und die Lehre des Mohammad* (Berlin, 1861–5), vol. III, p. 457. Mary H. Kingsley, *Travels in West Africa* (London, 1897), p. 451. See Marillier, *op. cit.* n. 2 above, p. 222, etc.

214. Stengel, *GK*, p. 121. C. Michel, *Recueil d'Inscriptions grecques* (Brussels, 1900), 714, 37 (Mykonos). Cf. Martin J. Hall, *Through My Spectacles in Uganda* (London, 1898), pp. 96, 97 (Baganda).

215. Athenaeus, VI, 261D.

216. Smith, *RS*, pp. 435ff. Cf. C. O. Müller, *Denkmäler der alten Kunst* (Göttingen, 1832), I, pl. lix, 299b, illustration of Hera Αἰγοφάγος.

217. e.g., at Thebes, Herodotus, II, 42.

218. Varro, *De Re Rustica*, I, 29, 3.

219. Levit. i, 6, 8, 9; ix, 13. Exod. xxix, 17. The bones must not be broken: Exod. xii, 46. Numb. ix, 12.

220. Levit. vii, 14; ix, 21; x, 14, 15; xiv, 12, 21.

221. See above, p. 36. We recall the Biblical prohibitions against eating blood, which is life, and which belongs to God. I Sam. xiv, 32, 33; Deut. xii, 23; Levit. xvii, 11; Gen. ix, 2–5. Cf. Virgil, *Georgics*, II, 484; Servius on *Aeneid*, III, 67; V, 78; cf. A. B. Ellis, *The Ewe-speaking Peoples of the Slave Coast* (London, 1890), p. 112. Cf. Marillier, *op. cit.* n. 2 above, p. 351.

222. Levit. iii, 3, 4, 16ff; vii, 23; ix, 19, 20; for the *shelamim*, Levit. iv, 8ff, 19, 31; ix, 10. In Greece, Stengel, *GK*, p. 101; Paton, *Cos*, 38; Hesychius, ἔνδρατα; Herodotus, IV, 62.

223. Levit. i, 9, 13, 17; ii, 2, 9, etc.; Psalm lxv (lxvi), 15. Cf. Isa. i, 13. Cf. Clermont-Ganneau, *op. cit.* n. 42 above, p. 599. *Iliad*, I, 317; VIII, 549ff.

224. Levit. xxi, 8, 17, 21. Ezek. xliv, 7. Herodotus, IV, 61. Cf. for the Hirpi Sorani and the way in which the wolves carried off the meat of sacrifices, Mannhardt, *WFK*, II, p. 332.

225. *Odyssey*, III, 51ff, VII, 201ff.

226. In the Hebrew ritual the victim was either boiled or

burnt. For the victims that were boiled, see I Sam. ii, 13; Herodotus, IV, 61.

227. See above, p. 26.

228. Exod. xxix, 32ff; Levit. vii, 8, 14; I Sam. ii, 13ff; Ezek. xliv, 29. *C.I.S.* 165 passim, 26.

229. Levit. x, 16ff, cf. iv, 11; vi, 18ff.

230. The difference was resolved by making a distinction: the victim had to be burnt 'outside the camp' when the blood had been brought into the sanctuary, that is, at the sacrifice of the Day of Atonement. In other cases the flesh belonged to the priests. Levit. vi, 23; x, 18; cf. iv, 21; viii, 17; iv, 11.

231. Cf. Act. Fr. Arv. a 218 (*Corpus Inscr. Lat.*, VI, 2104), *et porcilias piaculares epulati sunt et sanguinem postea.* Servius on *Aeneid*, III, 231.

232. Exod. xxix, 27ff; Levit. vii, 13, 29ff; x, 14. Numb. v, 9; vi, 20; xviii, 8ff; Deut. xviii, 3.

233. Levit. vi, 19, 22. Only men could eat of the *hattat*, and they had to be pure. For the *shelamim* (x, 14) the wives of the Cohanim were admitted, but these had to be eaten in a pure place. The meats are always cooked in a sacred room: Ezek. xlvi, 20.

234. Paton, *Cos*, 37, 21, 51; 38, 2, 5; 39, 10ff. Michel, *op. cit.* n. 214 above, 714 (Mykonos), 726 (Miletus). G. Doublet, 'Inscriptions du Paphlagonie', *Bulletin de correspondance hellénique*,.1889, p. 300 (Sinope). Pausanias, V, 13, 2. P. Stengel, 'Zunge des Opfertiers', *Jahrbuch für Philologie*, 1879, pp. 687ff.

235. Rohde, *Psyche* (Engl. trans.), p. 257.

236. Herodotus, IV, 161; VI, 57.

237. Paton, *Cos*, 38, 17.

238. Plutarch, *Quaestiones convivales*, VI, 8, 1 (Smyrna); Virgil, *Aeneid*, VI, 253. Servius, ad loc. Cf. Tautain, in *Anthropologie*, 1897, p. 670. The Septuagint here translates 'olah by holocaust.

239. Levit. i, 9; ix, 14; ix, 20; i, 17. Ezek. xl, 38.

240. Deut. xxxiii, 10; 'olah kalil, I Sam. vii, 9; Ps. l (li), 21; the kalil is distinguished from the 'olah.

241. Lucian, *De dea syria*, 58; Herodian, V, 5ff. Lampridius, *Elagabalus*, 8. F. C. Movers, *Die Phönizier* (Bonn, 1841), I, 365. Plutarch, *De Iside et Osiride*, 30. At the Thargelia: Ammonius, p. 142 Valck.; cf. Mannhardt, *MythForsch*, p. 136, n. 1. At the Thesmophoria: E. Rohde, 'Unedirte Lucianscholien . . .', *Rheinisches Museum* (N.F. XXV, 1870), 549 (Scholium on Lucian, *Dial. meretr.*, II, 1). At Marseilles: Servius on *Aeneid*, III, 57. The goat of Azazel, on the day of the Atonement, was likewise

thrown down from the top of a rock. (Talm. Babl., *Yoma*, Mishnah, 67a.)

242. There is some analogy between these castings down of the victim and the drownings practised at the agrarian festivals. See Stengel, *GK*, pp. 120ff. Mannhardt, *WFK*, II, pp. 278, 287. Cf. Rohde, *Psyche*, I, 192.

243. Levit. xvi, 22.

244. Strabo, X, 2, 9.

245. Levit. xiv, 53.

246. Plutarch, *Quaestiones convivales*, VI, 8, 1. For some facts of the same kind, the number of which could easily be increased, see Frazer, *GB*, II, pp. 157ff.

247. Levit. ix, 22. The *ShB* wonderfully expresses the same principle: 'the sacrifice belongs to the gods, the blessing to the sacrifier.' *ShB*, 2, 3, 4, 5.

248. Levit. xiv. 7. Wellhausen, *op. cit.* n. 85 above, p. 174 (initiation). In Greece, Xenophon, *Anabasis*, II, 2, 9 (oath). Frazer, *Pausanias*, III, p. 277, p. 593 (purification).

249. Lucian, *De dea syria*, 55. Pausanias, I, 34, 5 (lying down on the skin of the victim). Cf. Frazer, *Pausanias*, II, p. 476. Διὸς κῴδιον. Stengel, *GK*, p. 146. Cf. J. de Witte, 'L'Expiation ou la purification de Thésée', *Gazette archéologique* (Paris), vol. 9 (1884), p. 352. Smith, *RS*, pp. 437, 438.

250. Smith, *RS*, pp. 383-4.

251. Ashes of the red heifer which are used as lustration waters. Numb. xix, 9. Ovid, *Fasti*, IV, 639, 725, 733.

252. See above, Jer. xxxiv, 18ff.; cf. I Kings, xviii, 32. The rite seems to have been a part of a sacramentary sacrifice, symbolical of a contract. Cf. Gen. xiii, 9ff. Plutarch, *Quaestiones Romanae*, 111.

253. It is known that the technical name of the flesh of the *zebah shelamim*, etc., that could be consumed in Jerusalem was *Kodashim* (sanctities). (Cf. Septuagint, κρία ἅγια). Jer. xi, 15. Cf. Smith, *RS*, p. 238.

254. In the *zebah shelamim*, except for the reserved portions, the sacrifier is entitled to everything.

255. See Smith, *RS*, pp. 237ff.

256. Levit. vii, 15–18; xix, 5–8; Exod. xxix, 34. Cf. Mannhardt, *WFK*, II, p. 250. Frazer, *GB*, II, p. 70.

257. Levit. vii, 15; xxii, 29, 30. See Dillmann-Knobel, vol. XII, p. 448.

258. Exod. xii, 10; xxiii, 18; xxxiv, 25; Deut. xvi. 4.

259. Pausanias, X, 388; see Frazer, *Pausanias*, III, p. 240.
Smith, *RS*, pp. 282, 369. Cf. Athenaeus, VII, 276.

260. Pausanias, II, 27, 1; X, 38–8. Hesychius, s.v. 'Εστία
Θύομεν. Paton, *Cos*, 38, 24.

261. Pausanias, X, 32–9 (cult of Isis at Tithorea). The remains
of the victim were exhibited in the sanctuary from one festival
to another; and before each festival they were taken away and
buried.

262. Levit. vi, 4; xiv, 4; cf. iv. 11; the blood of the birds killed
in the temple was covered with earth. At Olympia there was a
· heap of ashes before the altar: Pausanias, V, 13, 8; see Frazer,
Pausanias, III, 566; Stengel, *GK*, p. 15.

263. The wife of the sacrifier is present at all the Hindu solemn
sacrifices, standing in a special place, loosely bound, and is the
object of certain rites, which communicate to her in some degree
the emanations of the sacrifice and assure her fertility. *KShS*, VI,
6, 1ff; *ApShS*, III, 18, 1, 12 com.

264. She causes the animal to drink at every gasp for breath,
sarvan pranan (*ApShS*, VII, 18, 6), while the officiant sprinkles the
animal's limbs liberally with water (*TS*, 1, 3, 9, 1. Cf. 6, 3, 9, 1;
VS, VI, 14; *ShB*, 3, 8, 2, 4, 7); in *TS nasike*, etc., must be recon-
stituted. The ceremony has several meanings. The Taittiriyins
emphasize its propitiatory nature: death is a 'pain', a flame, which
burns with each gasp for breath and must be appeased. For this
reason, at each gasp water is given it to drink, and the pain and
the flame disappear with the water into the earth. (Cf. *ShB*, 3, 8,
2, 8 and 16). Thus the Taittiriyins put for each one of the mantras
addressed to each orifice of the animal, 'Drink', and not 'Purify
yourself' (*VS*), the expression which corresponds to the name of
the rite. The explanation of the Vajasaneyins insists on the purificatory nature of the rite; they say 'Purify yourselves'; the victim
is a life, it is even the *amrita* (immortal food, immortality) of the
gods. Now the animal is killed when it is suffocated and appeased.
'But the waters are the breaths of life (they contain the vital
principle); thus, by performing this (this lustration), the breaths
are replaced. The victim becomes life and the immortal food of
the immortals.' (*ShB, loc. cit.*)

265. *ApShS*, VII, 18, 14, mantras; *TS*, 1, 3, 9, 2; see *ibid.*, 6,
3, 9, 2, proposes a more exact rite (cf. *KShS*, VI, 6, 11). But the
texts of the school of the Rig Veda (the *adhrigunigada*, *AshvShS*,
III, 3, 1; *AitB*, 6, 7, 1, 10) simply speak of sprinkling the blood in
order to repel the evil spirits. The discussion that takes place about

this subject is interesting; it is explained that the evil spirits, like the gods, are present at sacrifices; they also must have their share, since otherwise, as they have a right to it, if they were not given it to make them go away (*nir-ava-da*): cf. Oldenberg, *RelV*, p. 218, and *TS*, 6, 3, 9, 2), they would 'weigh heavily' on the sacrifier and his family. Other different parts of the victim are thus attributed to the evil spirits. These are: the drops of blood which fall when the heart is being cooked (*KShS*, VI, 7, 13), and also the stomach, the excrements, and the blades of grass on which the blood that has been collected is spread. (*ApShS* does not give these details; see Schwab, *Thieropfer*, p. 137.) These are then all buried in the 'pit for excrements' outside the place of sacrifice (*ApShS*, VII, 16, 1; cf. *AshvShS*, III, 3, 1). The *AitB*, 6, 6, 16, gives another interpretation to this burial. The texts readily glide over these shares made over to evil spirits. It seemed an irreligious rite (cf. *AitB*, 6, 7, 2) to invite the enemies of the gods to the sacrifice. But the rites are plain: in general all that is left from the sacrifice that is unusable (for example, the husks of the corn ground to make a cake) are rejected and cast out in this way. To these facts may be compared the Greek practice of the sacrifice to Ἥρα γαμηλία in which the victim's gall was thrown away (Plutarch, *Conjugalia praecepta*, 27) and the Biblical prescription to bury the blood of the birds of purification. It is noteworthy that the ritual of the sacrifices of India shows that, contrary to accepted ideas, it is not necessarily the principle of a bloody sacrifice that the blood be made use of.

266. The upper portion of the peritoneum, muscular and fatty, 'the most juicy part from among the fatty parts, has been removed from the middle for you, and to you we give it', *RV*, III, 21, 5. It is the central portion of the animal, the principle of its individual life, its *atman* (*TS*, 6, 3, 9, 5), just as 'the blood is the life' with the Semites. It is the sacrificial principle of the victim (the *medhas*), *TS*, 3, 1, 5, 2; *ShB*, 3, 8, 2, 28; see *AitB*, 7, 3, 6, a curious ritual myth.

267. *ApShS*, VII, 19, 3ff. At the head walks a priest with a lighted torch in his hand, then follows the priest who carries the portion of the victim on two spits (for he must not touch it directly), then the sacrifier who holds the priest as described earlier (*ApShS*, VII, 19, 6, 7, comm.). The reasons for the rite are the same as are indicated above (see p. 33 and note 181). *TS*, 6, 3, 9, 3 and 4.

268. *RV*, III, 21, 5. Oldenberg's translation (*ad loc.*) against Sayana in *RV* and *TB*.

269. The whole rite is very ancient, for one of the priests recites the hymn: *RV*, II, 75, 1, then III, 21, in its entirety = *TB*, III, 6, 7, 1ff = *MS*, 3, 10, 1. Cf. *TS*, 6, 4, 3, 5. Cf. *AitB*, 7, 2, 5ff. See Ludwig, *Rig-Veda*, IV, p. 203. Bergaigne, *Histoire de la liturgie védique*, p. 18, considers this hymn a recent one, as it is made up of verses of varying metre, that is to say, a series of entirely separate formulas. (See Oldenberg, *Vedic Hymns*, Sacred Books of the East, XLVI, p. 283.) This fact is indisputable; the formulas come from diverse sources and were collected together comparatively late. But the formulas are very much earlier than the hymn. So much so that, although the hymn was not written as a unity, it appears as a unified whole in its object, and the natural way in which it has been made up shows that it is linked with one of the most ancient rites. The hymn describes very precisely all the details of the operation (cf. *TS*, 6, 3, 9, 5 and *ShB*, 3, 8, 2, 11). The Brahmins found a naturalist meaning in this sacrificial rite, which is among the most important.

270. *ApShS*, VII, 22, 2.

271. All of them wash. *ApShS*, VII, 22, 6=*KShS*, 6, 6, 29=*AshvShS*, 3, 5, 1 and 2. The mantras are *TS*, 4, 1, 5, 1=*RV*, X, 9, 1–3. The *VS*, VI, 16, gives the same text as *AV*, VI, 89. The last mantra expresses deliverance from sickness, sin, death, and from malediction, human and divine. It is moreover the sacrifice of the *vapa*, which, where the sacrifice has as its aim to redeem a man, marks the precise moment of redemption.

272. See Schwab, *Thieropfer*, no. 98, pp. 126ff.

273. See Schwab, *Thieropfer*, p. 141, no. 1. Cf. Ludwig, *Rig-Veda*, IV, p. 361. See *ApShS*, VII, 25, 7ff. *ShB*, 3, 8, 3, 10 (Sacred Books of the East, XXVI, 201). Eggeling *ad loc.*

274. *ApShS*, VII, 25, 8.

275. *TS*, 6, 3, 11, 1. During the sacrification is recited *RV*, VI, 60, 13; I, 109, 7 and 6=*TB*, 6, 3, 11, 1ff, which are formulas of glorification of the gods, and describe the way in which they accept the offering and consume it when it reaches them.

276. To Agni, who completes the rites (see Weber, *Indische Studien*, IX, p. 218) cf. Hillebrandt, *op. cit.* n. 28 above, p. 118. For the other creatures to whom are attributed shares (of the large intestine) in a supplementary offering (*ApShS*, VII, 26, 8ff), see Schwab, *Thieropfer*, no. 104. The mantras recited and the responses do not correspond very closely.

277. Other parts, without bones, can be added to them. *ApShS*, VII, 24, 11.

278. On the Ida, see especially Oldenberg, *RelV*, pp. 289ff, and the passages cited in his Index.

279. See Bergaigne, *op. cit.*, n. 131 above, I, pp. 323, 325; II, 92, 94. Lévi, *Sacrifice*, pp. 115ff.

280. This moment of sacrifice is important enough for the *ShB* to link up with it the famous classical legend of the flood. (*ShB*, 1, 8, 1, in its entirety; Eggeling, *ad loc.*, Sacred Books of the East, XII.) Cf. Weber, *Indische Studien*, I, pp. 8ff. Muir, *Old Sanskrit Texts*, I, pp. 182, 196ff. But the other Brahmanas have only the end of this legend, and only the end is an article of the Brahmin faith. According to them, it is by inventing the rite of the *Ida*, and thus creating the goddess Ida (his wife or his daughter, according to the texts) that Manu, the first man and the first sacrifier, acquired offspring and cattle. (See *TS*, 1, 7, 1 and 2, and 6 and 7 in their entirety; *TB*, 3, 7, 5, 6.) In any case, it and its corresponding material represent the animals, are their whole strength: *ida vai pashavo*, 'ida is the animals'.

281. See Hillebrandt, *NVO*, p. 124; Schwab, *Thieropfer*, p. 148.

282. Hillebrandt, *NVO*, p. 125.

283. The ceremony is called *idahvayana*, or *idopahvana*, a term which corresponds exactly to the epiclesis of the Christian Mass. The text is *AshvShS*, I, 7, 7, translated in Hillebrandt, *NVO*, pp. 125f; Oldenberg, *RelV*, pp. 290ff. The texts from *Shankhya Shrauta sutra*, I. 10, 1; *TB*, 3, 5, 8, 1; 3, 5, 13, 1ff are slightly different. This invocation consists essentially in a series of appeals to the divinity, which is thought to bring with it all the forces mentioned, and moreover to invite in its turn the priests and the sacrifier to take their share in the forces thus concentrated. During a pause the sacrifier says (*ApShS*, IV, 10, 6–*TS*, 1, 7, 1, 2), 'Let this offering' (of mingled milk) 'be my strength'.

284. *TB*, 3, 5, 8 *ad fin.*; 3, 5, 13 *ad fin.*

285. The *avantareda*, the supplementary *ida* that he holds in his other hand. (See Weber, *Indische Studien*, IX, p. 213.) He says (*AshvShS*, 1, 7, 8; cf. *TS*, 2, 6, 8, 1 and 2): 'Ida, accept our share, cause our cows to prosper, cause our horses to prosper. You have at your disposal the flower of wealth, feed us upon it, give us of it.'

286. The sacrifier says: 'Ida, accept, etc. . . . may we partake of you, partake in body and soul (commentary on *TB*), all of us with all our people.' (*TB*, 3, 7, 5, 6.)

287. *AshvShS*, I, 8, 2.

288. One school lays down a rite of presentation to the *manes*

Notes

(*KShS*, 3, 4, 16 and 17.) The rite, although an ancient one (*VS*, 11, 31) is only the rite of a school.

289. See the mantras in Hillebrandt, *NVO*, 126ff; it is in this way that the mouth of the *agnidhra* (fire priest) is supposed to be the very mouth of Agni. Thus the sacerdotal shares are indeed divine ones. There is no question here, as Oldenberg saw, of a meal taken in common, a rite of social communion, whatever may appear. In the *Ida* 'the share of the sacrifier' has a sort of 'medicating' power (Oldenberg); it gives strength to the sacrifier, 'it places the animals within him', as the texts have it: *pashun yajamane dadhati* (note the use of the locative). See *TS*, 2, 6, 7, 3; *AitB*, 2, 30, 1; 6, 10, 11; *ShB*, 1, 8, 1, 12, etc. The *ida* forms part of the ritual of the Hindu solemn sacrifices. We must add that what remains of the victim is to a certain extent profaned; the Brahmins and the sacrifier can take it home (Schwab, *Thieropfer*, p. 149). We know of no rules laying down the times allowed for eating the victims' remains. But some exist for the consumption of all kinds of food generally.

290. See above, p. 41.

291. It may cause surprise that in this scheme we have not mentioned those cases where the victim is not an animal. We might indeed have done so. We have seen, indeed, how the rituals proclaimed the equivalence of the two kinds of things (see above, p. 13). For example, in the whole of the agrarian sacrifices their basic identity makes possible the substitution of one for another (see p. 77). But there is more: it is possible to establish real symmetrical patterns between victims and sacrificial oblations. The preparation of the cakes, the way in which they were anointed with oil or butter, etc., corresponds to the preparation of the victim. Even the creation of the sacred thing during the course of the ceremony is much more evident in the case of oblation than in any other case, since it is often made entirely on the very place of sacrifice. (See for India: Hillebrandt, *op. cit.* n. 28 above, pp. 28, 41.) Particularly when they are figurines (see for India, Hillebrandt, *op. cit.* n. 10 above, sect. 64, p. 116; sect. 48. Cf. Weber, *Nakshatra*, II, 338—the information is rather fragmentary: *Sankh. grihya sutra*, IV, 19). For Greece, see above, p. 12. Stengel, *GK*, pp. 9off. Festus, 129; cf. Frazer, *GB*, II, pp. 84, 139ff. C. O. Lobeck, *Aglaophamus* (Königsberg, 1829), pp. 119, 1080ff. Next, the destruction has the same characteristic of definitive consecration as the putting to death of an animal victim. At least the spirit of the oblation is always removed outside the real world.

One difference only exists, natural because of the nature of things; in the majority of cases the moment of attribution and that of consecration coincide, without the victim having as such the character of something to be eliminated. Indeed, the libation is destroyed at the very moment when it falls upon the altar, is lost in the earth, evaporates or burns in the fire; the cake and the handful of flour are consumed and disappear in smoke. The sacrification and the attribution to the divinity make one single moment in the ritual. But there is no doubt about the nature of the destruction: thus the mere placing of wood to be burnt is, at certain moments, a sacrifice itself in the Hindu ritual. (We allude to the *samidheni*, see Hillebrandt, *NVO*, pp. 74ff.) Lastly the distribution of shares is, *mutatis mutandis*, analogous to that of the animal sacrifice: thus in the case of the sacrifice at the full or new moon, we find shares for the gods, an *ida*, etc. Let us finally recall that the most important of all the Hindu sacrifices, the most extraordinary case perhaps of all sacrifices, the one in which the victim is made to undergo all possible kinds of treatment, the sacrifice of the *soma* is, like the Christian sacrifice, made up of a vegetable oblation.

292. Nothing is easier to explain: for it is the same people and the same things that are in question, and, from another viewpoint, by virtue of the well-known laws that regulate religious matters, it is the same processes of lustration which bestow or remove a character of sacredness.

293. *ApShS*, VII, 26, 12; *KShS*, 6, 9, 11; *TS*, 1, 3, 11, 1 and *ShB*, 3, 8, 5, 5, for the mantra (*KShS* has made better use of it). A series of minor sacrifices have been made (see Schwab, *Thieropfer*, no. 111), the formulas for which express the ending of the rite.

294. *ApShS*, VII, 27, 4; *KShS*, VI, 9, 12. (It is remarkable that *ApShS* borrows the mantra from *VS*, VI, 21.)

295. Hillebrandt, *NVO*, pp. 145-7; Schwab, *Thieropfer*, 156-9. During this rite a curious recapitulation is made of the different moments of the sacrifice (*TB*, 3, 6, 15 in its entirety) and of the benefits that await the sacrifier; he will taste what he has given the gods to taste. (Cf. *AshvShS*, 1, 9, 1.)

296. Hillebrandt, *NVO*, pp. 147-9.

296. As he thanks him for having transported the offering to the gods: *ApShS*, VII, 28, 2; *TB*, 2, 4, 7, 11; cf. *TS*, 3, 5, 5, 4.

298. *ApShS*, ibid., 4. *AitB*, 6, 3, 5.

299. Schwab, *Thieropfer*, p. 107. Hillebrandt, *NVO*, pp. 140f.

300. *ApShS*, VII, 26, 15; *ShB*, 3, 8, 5, 8; *TS*, 6, 4, 1, 8; *TS*, 1, 3, 11; *VS*, VI, 22; *ApShS*, VII, 27, 16.

Notes

301. *ApShS*, 26, 16ff; *TS*, 1, 4, 45, 3.
302. Hillebrandt, *NVO*, p. 174. Cf. Lévi, *Sacrifice*, p. 66.
303. Cf. *ShB*, 1, 1, 1, 4–7.
304. *Avabhrita*. See Weber, *Indische Studien*, X, 393ff. Cf. Oldenberg, *RelV*, pp. 407ff. Perhaps the expressions 'fluid', etc., used by Oldenberg are not the best, but he has nevertheless indicated the meaning of the rite as it appears to be—not in the *RV*, where it is moreover mentioned (see Grassmann, *Wörterbuch zum Rig-Veda, ad verb.*), but in all the other ritual and theological texts. *ApShS*, VIII, 7, 12ff, and XIII, 19ff. *KShS*, VI, 10, 1; X, 8, 16ff.
305. These places, the ponds, the *tirthas*, which even today in India are particularly sacred spots, are alleged to be the favourite possession of Varuna. (*ShB*, 4, 4, 5, 10.)
306. *ApShS*, XIII, 20, 10, 11.
307. *ApShS*, XIII, 22, 2 com. At the same time they repeat various formulas which explain that they are expiating their sins, their ritual errors, that they are acquiring strength, prosperity and glory, by assimilating to themselves in this way the magic force of the waters, the rites, and the plants.
308. They give their old garments to the priests, thus abandoning their former personality, and by putting on new ones they are acquiring 'a new skin like a serpent'. 'There is now no more sin in them than in a toothless infant.' *ShB*, 4, 4, 5, 23.
309. Levit. xvi, 22, 23. He changed his garb yet again after having ceased to fast, and returned home to receive the congratulations of his friends for having borne up under all the trials, accomplished all the rites and escaped all the dangers of that day. (Talmud Babl., *Yoma*, Mishnah, 70a.)
310. Levit. xvi. 26.
311. Levit. xvi, 28. As likewise did he who brought back the ashes of the red heifer.
312. We know from Ezek. xliv, 19, that the garments of the priests were shut away in 'holy rooms', to which priests went to dress and undress before going out to the people; contact with these garments was dangerous for the laity.
313. Porphyry, *De Abstinentia*, II, 44. Paton, *Cos*, 38, 24. Cf. Frazer, *GB*, II, pp. 54ff.
314. Levit. vi, 21 (*hattat*).

Notes

CHAPTER THREE

315. Plato, *Republic*, VIII, 565D. Pausanias, VIII, 2, 6; VIII, 2, 3. Pliny, *Natural History*, VIII, 22. See Mannhardt, *WFK*, II, p. 340. There is the same legend about the sanctuary of Hyre. Gruppe, *Griechische Mythologie*, pp. 67ff. Cf. J. Wellhausen, *Reste Arabischen Heidentums*, p. 162 and note, p. 163. See below, p. 62.

316. We refer to the facts, well known since Mannhardt, Frazer, Sidney Hartland, under the name of 'external soul', with which the two latter authors have linked the whole theory of initiation.

317. Pausanias, V, 13, 3. The same prohibition at Pergamum for those who had sacrificed to Telephus.

318. See above, p. 40 and p. 43. It is strictly then that the identification sometimes sought between the sacrifier, the victim, and the god, is entirely realized. (On this principle, see Hebr. ii, 11.)

319. Psalm cv (cvi), 39. 'Thus they were defiled with their own works, and went a whoring with their own inventions.'

320. Levit. xiff. Cf. Marquardt, *op. cit.* n. 77 above, p. 277. Cf. Frazer, art. 'Taboo', *Encyclopedia Britannica* (9th edn.). Cf. Frazer, *GB*, *passim*. Cf. Jevons, *Introduction to the History of Religion*, pp. 107ff.

321. Cf. Rohde, *Psyche*, I, pp. 179, 192; S. R. Steinmetz, *Ethnologische Studien zur ersten Entwicklung der Strafe* (Leiden, 1894), II, pp. 350ff.

322. This is the usual punishment for ritual errors in Leviticus, Deuteronomy and Exodus, as in Ezekiel and the historical books; the rites must be observed if one does not want to die or be attacked with leprosy like king Uzziah. Cf. Oldenberg, *RelV*, pp. 287, 319. Cf. Bergaigne, *op. cit.* n. 131 above, III, pp. 150ff.

323. Levit. xvi. Cf. above, note 180.

324. Levit. xiv, 1ff.

325. For the Greek expiatory sacrifices see Lasaulx, *Sühnopfer der Griechen* (Würzburg, 1844), pp. 236ff; James Donaldson, 'On the Expiatory and Substitutionary Sacrifices of the Greeks', *Transactions of the Royal Society of Edinburgh* (1875-6), pp. 433ff. For the facts regarding the Germanic peoples, see Ulrich Jahn, *Die Abwehrenden und die Sühnopfer der Deutschen*, Inaug. Diss., Breslau, 1884, reprinted in K. Weinhold (ed.), *Germanistische Abhandlungen* (Breslau, 1884), III (*Die deutschen Opfergebräuche bei Ackerbau und Viehsucht*).

326. See Oldenberg, *RelV*, pp. 287ff, 522ff.

327. *KauS*, 26–18. Cf. Kuhn's fine article for a series of analogous rites in the whole of Europe (*Kuhns Zeitschrift*, XIII, pp. 113ff). On this rite see Bloomfield, *Hymns of the Atharva-Veda* (Sacred Books of the East, XLII), ad *AV*, i, 22, p. 264; cf. Introduction to VII, 116 (p. 565).

328. *AV*, I, 22, 4.

329. On the rites see Bloomfield, Sacred Books of the East, XLII, introduction to VII, 116 (p. 565), and M. Winternitz, 'Der Altindische Hochzeitsrituell', *Denkschriften der kaiserl. Akad. der Wissensch.*, *Phil.-hist. Kl.*, Vienna, XL (1892), pp. 6, 12, 23, 67. *KauS*, 18, 17, 16.

330. We translate literally. Bloomfield and the commentary explain (*ad loc.*) by the word 'crow'.

331. *AV*, VII, 115, 1.

332. *Lakshmi*, 'mark' of misfortune, the imprint of the goddess Nirriti (of destruction). This mark corresponds both to the black colour of the crow and to the small cake that is tied to its feet.

333. The casting of evil spells on the enemy is a constant theme of the Vedic, Atharvan, and other rituals.

334. Cf. *KauS*, 32, 17.

335. For this rite see Oldenberg, *RelV*, pp. 82, 446 n. 1, and above all Hillebrandt, *op. cit.* n. 10 above, p. 83. The rite forms part of the domestic ritual. The texts are: *Ashvalayana grihya Sutra*, 4, 8; *Parashara*, 3, 8; *Hiranyakeshin*, 2, 8, 9; *Apastamba grihyaSutra*, 19, 13ff; 201–19. The text of the *Ashv.* seems to attribute to this rite the meaning of a prosperity rite (4, 8, 35; *Parashara*, 3, 8, 2). But the characteristics of the rite are very clear and the commentary to *Hiranyakeshin*, 2, 9, 7 (Kirste ed., p. 153) sees it as a *shanti* to Rudra, king of the animals, a 'way of appeasing' the god by means of a victim who would be the 'spit-ox' (cf. Oldenberg's translation of *Hiranyakeshin*, Sacred Books of the East, XXX, p. 220). Oldenberg sees above all in this rite a case of animal fetishism. Thus he insists principally on developing the remarkable point of the rite, which is the incorporation of the god in the victim. The rite has come down to us only through fairly recent texts, which show considerable divergencies. We cannot give an historical analysis of them here. Our conclusion is that there were three more or less heterogeneous rites, which were combined either in pairs or all together according to the Brahmin schools and clans. We deal principally with the rite of the Atreya clans (*Ashv. Par.*). In any case the rite is a very ancient one, and the hymns of the *RV* to Rudra (V, 43; I, 114; II, 33; VII, 46) are, both by the Sutras

and by Sayana, devoted to this rite, to which they apply remarkably well.

336. On Rudra, see above all Oldenberg, *RelV*, 216-24, 283ff; 333ff. Cf. A. Barth, 'M. Oldenberg et la religion du Veda', *Journal des Savants* (Paris, 1896), pp. 133ff, 317ff, 389ff, 471ff. Bergaigne, op. cit. n. 131 above, III, 31ff; 152-4. Lévi, *Sacrifice*, p. 167 (*AitB*, 13, 9, 1). It is impossible for us to set out here the reasons for our explanations of the mythical personality of Rudra.

337. This is the point on which all the schools are in agreement: it is made to sniff the offerings (cf. Oldenberg, *RelV*, p. 82, and the way in which the divinized horse of the *ashvamedha* is made to inhale the offerings; cf. also *KShS*, 14, 3, 10). It is called by the whole series of Rudra's names; 'Om (the magic syllable) to Bhava, Om to Sharva, etc.,' cf. *AV*, IV, 28, and the texts to Rudra are recited: *TS*, 4, 5, 1ff. See *Mantrapatha of Apastamba*, ed. M. Winternitz, II, 18, 10ff.

338. According to Parashara.

339. No part of the animal can be brought back to the village 'because the god seeks to kill men.' The relatives could not approach the place of sacrifice, nor eat the flesh of the victim, without an order and a special invitation. *AshuShS*, 4, 8, 31 and 33 (see Oldenberg, Sacred Books of the East, XXIX, p. 258).

340. For simplicity of exposition it is everywhere to be understood that the same thing can be repeated, in the same terms of the objects.

341. Levit. xiv, 10ff.

342. Numb. vi, 13ff. Talmud Jerus., *Nazir* (Schwab trans., IX, pp. 84ff).

343. Talmud Jerus., *Nazir*, I, 2. The *nazir* offers the same sacrifice when he rids himself of his hair, which has become too heavy.

344. *Ibid.*, II, 10.

345. *Ibid.*, VI, 7 and 8. Numb. vi, 18.

346. Numb. vi, 19.

347. See especially Frazer, *GB*, additional note to vol. II, pp. 373ff, for some ethnographical facts; cf. *ibid.*, II, pp. 67ff. It would be easy to increase the number of facts cited. Frazer rightly saw that the majority of offerings of the firstfruits consist in the consecration of a part of the edible species, a part which represents the whole. But his analysis, which moreover he keeps on a factual level, did not take into account the function that was served by the rite in question.

348. This part is normally the first of everything. We recall the
extent of the Biblical prescriptions concerning the firstborn,
whether of men or of animals; the firstfruits and the first crops of
the year, the first products of a tree (*orlah*), the first wheat eaten
(*azymes*), the first dough leavened (*halla*). Of all that lives or
gives life, the firstfruits belong to Yahweh. The benedictions of
the Talmud and the synagogue further stress this notion, as they
are obligatory when a fruit is tasted for the first time, when a
meal is begun, etc.

349. Talmud Jerus., *Bikkurim*, III, Mishnah, 2ff. It is evident that
we cannot follow the rite in the Biblical texts, which contain only
the directions for the priests and not the popular usages. The
popular nature of all this rite is clear; the flute player, the bullock
crowned with olive, with gilded horns (which a kid with silvered
horns could replace, cf. Gemara, *ad loc.*), the baskets, the doves—
all these are original features of unquestionable antiquity. Moreover these texts of the Mishnah are themselves very ancient.

350. They met together the previous evening, and spent the
night in the public square (according to the Gemara, for fear of
impure contact).

351. Gemara *ad 2*. The rabbis discuss among themselves whether
it is as *shelamim* or as *'olah*.

352. A rite of personal redemption, a fairly remarkable case.

353. Cf. Talmud Babl., *Menahoth*, 58a (Schwab, *ad loc.*).

354. Numb. xix.

355. See above, p. 53.

356. ·Ritual of Kippur.

357. Talmud Jerus., *Maaser Sheni*, VI, Gemara (see Schwab,
p. 247). Cf. *Middoth*, Mishnah, quoted *ibid.*

CHAPTER FOUR

358. It is well known that this 'death' into which the devotee is
plunged before the return of Yahweh is a basic theme of the
Prophets and the Psalms. (Cf. Ezek. xxxvii, 2; Job xxxiii, 28, and
the commentary in Talmud Jerus., *Baba Kamma*, Gemara, VII,
8 (4)). See the whole of Psalm cxiv–cxv (cxvi) and cxvii (cxviii)
from verse 17. 'I shall not die, but live,' etc. We need not remind
readers of the Catholic formulas in the Mass.

359. In India, the whole world of sacrifice is considered to be
this new world. When the sacrifier who has been seated is raised
up, he is told: 'Stand up, into life.' While they walk bearing a

sacred object, the formula runs: 'Go the length of the vast atmosphere' (*TS*, 1, 1, 2, 1). At the beginning of every rite one of the first mantras is: 'Thou for the juice, thou for the sap.' (*TS*, 1, 1, 1, 1.) And at the end of the sacrifice the process of regeneration is complete (cf. above, p. 47, n. 308).

360. Pausanias, II, 24, 1. For the transport induced by the soma, and the way in which the *rishis* who have drunk it feel themselves either carried off into the other world or possessed by the god Soma, see Bergaigne, *op. cit.* n. 131 above, I, 151ff; *RV*, X, 119; X, 136, 3, 6ff; VIII, 48 in its entirety. Cf. Oldenberg, *Religion der Veda*, p. 530. For possession see G. A. Wilken, 'Het shamanisme bij de volken van den Indischen Archipel', extract from *Bijdragen tot de taal-, land- en volkenkunde van Nederlandsch Indië*, 1887, pp. 427ff. Frazer, *Pausanias*, V, p. 381; cf. Pausanias, I, 34, 3. W. H. Roscher, 'Die "Hundekrankheit" der Pandareostöchter und andere mythische Krankheiten', *Rheinisches Museum*, LIII, pp. 172ff.

361. These expressions are borrowed from the Biblical and Talmudic speculations on the day of 'judgement', of Kippur.

362. See our reviews of the books of A. Nutt, Rohde and Cheetham, in *Année sociologique*, II (1899), pp. 214ff. On the Hindu doctrines, see Lévi, *Sacrifice*, 102, 108, 161. On the *haoma*, see J. Darmesteter, *Haurvatat et Ameretat* (Paris, 1875), p. 54; *Ormazd et Ahriman* (Paris, 1875), p. 90.

363. See E. Lefébure in *Mélusine* (cf. n. 176 above), cols. 146ff; D. G. Brinton, *Religions of Primitive Peoples*, pp. 89ff.

364. The pilgrim of Mecca, the ancient sacrifier of the *hajj*, took and still takes the title *haji*. See Wellhausen, *Reste Arabischen Heidentums*, p. 80.

365. See Duchesne, *Christian Worship* (Eng. trans., 1919 edn.), pp. 308ff. See above, p. 52. On the relation between the sacrifice and the rites of initiation and the introduction of the new soul, see Frazer, *GB*, I, 344ff. The entry into the Christian life has always been considered as a real change of nature.

366. We know that in many parallel cases, and even here, another result is intended: to outwit evil spirits by changing one's name, to baffle bad luck. See *Midrash on Eccl.*, V, 5, par. 1; Talmud Babl., *Rosh Hashanah*, 16b; Talmud Jerus., *Shebuoth*, Gemara, VI, 10 (Schwab trans., IV, p. 79). Cf. C. Snouck Hurgronje, *Mekka in the Later Part of the 19th Century*, trans. J. H. Monahan (Leiden and London, 1931), p. 99.

367. Talmud Jerus., *Gittin*, Gemara, p. 45 (Schwab).

368. See W. Caland, *Altindischen Todten- und Bestattungs-gebräuche* (1896), no. 2. J. J. M. de Groot, *The Religious System of China* (1892), I, p. 5.

369. See reviews, *Année sociologique* (1899), p. 217.

370. *Sacrifice*, pp. 93–5. We adhere entirely to the comparison proposed by Lévi between the Brahmin theory of escape from death by sacrifice and the Buddhist theory of *moksha*, deliverance. Cf. H. Oldenberg, *Le Bouddha* (Paris, 1934), pp. 48ff.

371. See Bergaigne, *op. cit.* n. 131 above, for the *amritam*, the 'immortal essence' conferred by the soma (I, pp. 254ff). But in it, as in Hillebrandt, *Vedische Mythologie* (n. 32 above), I, p. 289 *et passim*, the interpretations of pure mythology have encroached somewhat on the explanations of the texts. See A. Kuhn, *Herab-kunft des Feuers und des Göttertranks* (1886). Cf. W. H. Roscher, *Nektar und Ambrosia* (Leipzig, 1883).

372. See Darmesteter, *Haurvatat et Ameretat*, pp. 16, 41.

373. In dogma (e.g., Irenaeus, *Adversus Haereses*, IV, 4, 8, 5) as well as in the best-known rites. Thus the consecration of the Host is effected by a formula in which the effect of sacrifice upon salvation is mentioned. See F. Magani, *Antica liturgia romana* (Milan, 1898), II, p. 268, etc. With these facts might also be compared the Talmudic *Haggadah* according to which the tribes that vanished in the desert and have not performed sacrifice will have no part in eternal life (Talmud Jerus., *Sanhedrin*, Gemara, X, 4, 5 and 6), nor will the people of a city laid under interdict for having given itself over to idolatry, nor will the impious Korah. This Talmudic passage is based on Psalm xlix (l), 5: 'Gather my saints together unto me, those that have made a covenant with me by sacrifice.'

374. This might be the place to study the political side, so to speak, of sacrifice. In a fair number of politico-religious societies (secret societies in Melanesia and Guinea, Brahminism, etc.), the social hierarchy is often determined by the qualities each individual acquires in the course of sacrifice. It would also be appropriate to consider the cases where it is the group (family, corporation, society, etc.) which is the sacrifier, and to see what are the effects produced on an entity of this kind by sacrifice. It would be easy to see that all these sacrifices, of sacralization or desacralization, have, other things being equal, the same effects on society as on the individual. But the question falls rather within the sphere of general sociology than in an exact study of sacrifice. Besides, it has been closely studied by English anthropologists: the effect of sacrificial communion on society is one of their favourite topics. See

Smith, *RS*, pp. 284ff; E. Sidney Hartland, *The Legend of Perseus*, II, chap. xi, etc.

375. Grant Allen, in the second part of his *The Evolution of the Idea of God* (London, 1897), has advanced ideas concerning these sacrifices and the sacrifices of the God which will perhaps appear relatively analogous to our own (see especially pp. 265, 266, 339, 340ff). We hope, however, that fundamental differences will be noticed also.

376. It is one of the rites the comparative study of which is most advanced. See H. Gaidoz, *Les Rites de la Construction* (Paris, 1882); R. Winternitz, 'Einige Bemerkungen über das Bauopfer bei den Indern' (*Mitteilungen der Anthropologischen Gesellschaft zu Wien*, XVII (1887), Introd., pp. [37]ff. Also especially the exhaustive monograph of P. Sartori, 'Über das Bauopfer', in *Zeitschrift für Ethnographie*, XXX (1898), with its classification of the forms, in which only the analysis of the rite leaves anything to be desired. For the preservation of the bodies or parts of the bodies of the victims in building, see G. Wilken, 'Iets over de schedelvereering bij de volken van den Indischen Archipel' (*Bijdragen tot de taal-, land-, en volkenkunde van Nederlandsch Indië*, XXXVIII, 1889); Pinza, *Conservazione delle teste umane, passim*.

377. This is the most common case. In reality it is a matter of creating a kind of god to whom worship will later be paid. This is a case parallel to that of the agrarian sacrifice. This spirit will be vague or precise, will be fused with the force that makes the building solid or will become a sort of personal god, or will be both at the same time. But it will always be linked by certain ties to the victim out of which it proceeds and to the building of which it is the guardian and protector, against spells, illnesses, and misfortunes, inspiring respect for the threshold in all, whether thieves or inmates. (H. C. Trumbull, *The Threshold Covenant*, 1896.) In the same way as the agrarian victim is 'fixed' by sowing its remains, so blood is spread over the foundations and later the head is walled up. The construction sacrifice could be repeated later in various rituals—firstly on grave occasions such as the repair of a building or the siege of a town; then it became periodic and was in many cases mixed up with agrarian sacrifices and, like them, gave rise to the creation of mythical personages. See F. Dümmler, 'Sitten-geschichtliche Parallelen', *Philologus*, LVI (1897), pp. 19ff.

378. This is also a very common case. Here it is a matter of redemption, through a victim, from the anger of the spirit that is the owner of the ground, or in some cases of the building itself.

In India the two rites are found combined (see Winternitz, *loc. cit.*) in the sacrifice to Vastoshpati, 'Rudra, Lord of the place'; normally they are separate. (Sartori, *op. cit.* (n. 376 above), pp. 14, 15, 19, 42ff.)

379. See Winternitz, *loc. cit.*

380. The best known case is that of Jephthah's daughter. But after the accomplishment of a voluntary sacrifice there is always the feeling of having fulfilled one's obligations, of having 'shifted' the vow' as the Hindu theologians forcibly put it.

381. The general formula of attribution which the sacrifier uttered when the officiant cast any part into the fire ran in Vedic India as follows: 'This to the god N.N., and not to me.'

382. These are the sacrifices 'of thanksgiving', of praise, of the Bible. They seem in most religions to have been relatively few. For India, see Oldenberg, *Religion der Veda*, pp. 305, 306; Wilken, 'Over eene nieuwe theorie des Offers', *De Gids*, 1890, pp. 365ff.

383. H. Callaway, *The Religious System of the Amazulu* (Springvale, Natal, 1868), p. 59, n. 14. Cf. Frazer, *GB*, II, 42, etc. Cf. Marillier, *Revue d'histoire des religions*, XXXVII (1898), p. 209. Cf. Bernardino de Sahagun, *Historia de las cosas de Nueva España*, II, p. 20.

384. Hillebrandt, *op. cit.* n. 10 above, p. 75. With these facts must be compared the cases of drowning victims in water. In other cases water is poured over any victim: I Kings xviii, 19ff, etc. Cf. Krahmer, 'Das Fest "Sinsja" und das Feldgebet', etc., *Globus*, LXXIII (1898), p. 165. Cf. Smirnov and Boyer, *Populations finnoises* (1898), p. 175.

385. In the Vedic ritual, when the animal is anointed on the croup, is said: 'May the Lord of the sacrifice (the sacrifier) go with (you and) his will to heaven' (*ApShS*, VII, 14, 1; *VS*, 6, 10, 6; *TS* 1, 3, 8, 1), which is commented upon in *TS*, 6, 3, 7, 4; *ShB*, 3, 7, 4, 8, where it is explained that the animal is going off to heaven and bears off on its croup the prayer of the sacrifier. The victim has often been imagined as a messenger of mankind, as with the Mexicans and the Thracians of Herodotus (IV, 9, etc.). Our enumeration of objective sacrifices is by no means complete; we have not dealt with the divinatory sacrifice, the sacrifice of imprecation, the food sacrifice, or the sacrifice of the oath, etc. A study of these various forms would perhaps reveal that in them also there is question of creating and utilizing a sacred thing, a spirit directed towards such and such a thing. Perhaps from this viewpoint it will be possible to arrive at a classification.

Notes

386. See Mannhardt, *MythForsch*, pp. 68ff. Smith, *RS*, pp. 304ff. Frazer, *GB*, II, pp. 38, 41. H. von Prott, 'Buphorien', in *Rheinisches Museum*, 1897, pp. 187ff. Stengel, *GK*, pp. 399ff. L. R. Farnell, *Cults of the Greek States*, I, pp. 56, 58, 88ff (he sees in the Bouphonia an instance of the totemic cult). Frazer, *Pausanias*, II, pp. 303ff; V, p. 509. A. Mommsen, *Heortologie* (1864), pp. 512ff. Gruppe, *Griechische Mythologie*, I, p. 29.
387. See Pausanias, I, 24, 4; 28, 10. Porphyry, *De abstinentia*, II, 9; 28ff. Scholiast on Aristophanes, *Nubes*, 985. Scholion on Iliad, XVIII, 83. Suidas, Διὸς ψῆφος. Hesychius, Διὸς θᾶκοι.
388. Pausanias, I, 24, 4.
389. Porphyry, *De abstinentia*, II, 28.
390. Porphyry, *De abstinentia*, II, 29; II, 28, 30. Scholion on Homer, *l.c.* Scholion on Aristophanes, *l.c.*
391. Eusebius, *Praeparatio Evangelica*, III, 11, 12, saw in the death of Adonis the symbol of the reaped crops. But this is to make of the rite a vague and narrow idea.
392. Mommsen, *loc. cit.* (n. 386 above) believes that the Bouphonia was a threshing festival.
393. Stengel, *GK*, p. 216. claims that the superposing of the sacrifice of blood on the offering of the firstfruits in the Diipolia is a case of substitution of the blood sacrifice for vegetable offerings.
394. Cato, *De Agricultura*, 14. Ambarvalia: Marquardt, *op. cit.* n. 77 above, p. 200, n. 3. Cf. Frazer, *GB*, I, p. 39. See some very clear examples of the same kind of facts in Sartori, 'Bauopfer' (n. 376 above), p. 17, and Pinza, *op. cit.* n. 376 above, p. 154.
395. There was a confession at the bringing of the tithe and the fruits into the temple at Jerusalem. Talmud Jerus., *Ma'aser Sheni*, Mishnah, V, 10. In India a confession by the woman was part of the ritual of the *Varunapraghasas*. Lévi, *Sacrifice*, p. 156.
396. J. Wellhausen, *Prolegomena zu Geschichte Israels* (Berlin, 1886), ch. III, par. 1. Smith, *RS*, pp. 406, 464, etc. In opposition to the over-narrow interpretation of Wellhausen and Smith, we maintain that the festival has the characteristic of communion. The way in which the first ear of corn is consumed must be noted, as well as that in which the first sheaf is consecrated. We must say that here as elsewhere there is simply a case of a naturally complex rite, without there necessarily being any question of a fusion of rites of different origin and nationality.
397. The obligation to sacrifice the Passover, to consume the lamb, to bring the firstfruits (see above, n. 330, cf. p. 70) is in the Hebrew ritual a strictly personal one. In the same way, in the

148

rite of the *Varunapraghasas*, studied later on, we find a remarkable instance of personal redemption. From each individual member of the family is unloosed the 'bond' with which Varuna might tie him. As many barley cakes are made in the form of pots (*karambhapatrani*) as there are members of the family (*ApShS*, VIII, 5, 41), plus one extra, which represents the child to be born (*TB*, 1, 6, 5, 5) and at a certain moment of the ceremony everyone places them on his head (*ApShS*, VIII, 6, 23). In this way, says the Brahmana, Varuna, the god of the barley, is driven away from one's head (*TB*, 1, 6, 5, 4).

398. See Pausanias, II, 32, 2 (Troezen). Cf. Frazer, *Pausanias*, III, pp. 266ff. Pausanias, III, 11, 2; 14, 8 and 10; 19, 7 (Sparta). H. Usener, 'Der Stoff der griechischen Epos', *SitzBer. d. k. Akad. d. Wiss. in Wien, Phil.-hist. Kl.*, CXXXVII (1898), pp. 42ff. Cf. Mannhardt, *WFK*, I, p. 281. Frazer, *GB*, II, 165. On the combats at the Holi festivals, see W. Crooke, *Popular Religions and Folklore of Northern India* (Westminster, 1896), II, pp. 315ff., where some equivalent phenomena will be found cited. But the rite is a complex one, and it is very possible that there is in particular here a magic imitation of the annual struggle between the good and evil spirits.

399. The legend indeed marks the almost expiatory character of the Bouphonia.

400. L. F. Farnell, *op. cit.*, n. 386, and Robertson Smith, *Encyclopedia Britannica*, 9th edn., art. 'Sacrifice', see in it a survival of totemic communion.

401. Porphyry, *loc. cit.*

402. Mannhardt, *WFK*, I, 105. Frazer, *GB*, II, pp. 71, 106, 157; additional note to vol. II.

403. Cf. Frazer, *GB*, II, pp. 9, 21, 23, 31, 42, 73, 75, 78, etc.

404. Frazer, *GB*, II, p. 74.

405. The Hebrews could not eat of the fruits of the Promised Land until they had eaten of the unleavened bread and the lamb. Jos. v, 10ff. Exod. xii, 15ff; xxxiv, 18, etc.

406. Frazer, *GB*, II, p. 31.

407. According to the text of the words of the Pythian oracle, it seems that communion was relatively supererogatory (λῷον ἔσεσθαι).

408. See Lévi, *Sacrifice*, p. 155, n. 5.

409. Hence the name of the rite, 'the foods of Varuna'.

410. *ShB*, 2, 5, 2, 1. See Lévi, *Sacrifice*, p. 156, no. 1. The text *TB*, 1, 6, 4, 1, indicates only this last phase of the myth. We are studying only one of the three rites that go to make up the

Notes

ceremony; one of these is a bath identical with the bath of the exit from the sacrifice to soma (see above, p. 47); the other is a confession by the woman comparable in every respect to the Levite testing of the adulterous woman. Thus the whole festival has a very marked purificatory nature. (See above, p. 63, notes 362 and 364.)

411. All made from barley; in exceptional cases some may be made from rice. *ApShS*, VIII, 5, 35.

412. *ApShS*, VIII, 5, 42; 6, 1ff; 10ff. Evidently these two images represent the spirit of the barley, considered as fertilizing and fertilized (cf. *TB*, 1, 6, 4, 4, on the figurative copulation of these two animals, by means of which the creatures are freed from the ties of Varuna), but there is no very clear text on this point; and although the rite indeed has in itself the meaning of a magical creation of the spirit of the barley (cf. *ShB*, 2, 5, 2, 16, where it is said that the ram is 'Varuna visible' and where a figurative ram is concerned, and not any ram, as Lévi believes, *Sacrifice*, p. 155, n. 4), the texts do not develop this meaning sufficiently for us to enlarge upon it.

413. *Ava-yaj* (*TB*, 1, 6, 5, 1.)

414. Mannhardt, *WFK*, I, pp. 350ff.

415. Macpherson, *Memorials of Service in India*, pp. 129ff. Cf. the sacrifice of the bullock in the fields, *GB*, II, 20, 23, 41.

416. Mannhardt, *WFK*, I, p. 363.

417. Bahlmann, *Münsterländische Märchen*, p. 294.

418. Höfler, *op. cit.* n. 95 above, 4.

419. Frazer, *GB*, II, pp. 21, 28ff., 43, 47ff.

420. Mannhardt, *WFK*, I, pp. 350ff. Frazer, *GB*, I, pp. 381ff.

421. In winter the spirit lived on the farm. Frazer, *GB*, II, pp. 16, 14.

422. Cf. Kondakof, *op. cit.* n. 203 above, p. 181 (Tribes of the Altai). Herodotus, IV, 72. Frazer, *GB*, II, p. 42 (China). *Ibid.*, pp. 94, 220, for similar usages.

423. Frazer, *GB*, II, p. 220.

424. *Ibid.*, I, p. 266.

425. *Ibid.*, I, pp. 257ff.

426. Ovid, *Fasti*, IV, 731ff. Propertius, IV, 1, 19. Mannhardt, *WFK*, II, pp. 314ff; *MythForsch*, p. 189.

427. Ovid, *Fasti*, IV, 639.

428. Frazer, *GB*, II, p. 45. Scholium to Lucian in *Rheinisches Museum*, NF XXV (1870), pp. 548ff (Rohde). Cf. the cult of Isis at Tithorea; see above, p. 41, n. 261.

429. See Marillier, *op. cit.* n. 2 above, p. 209; II Kings xviii, 19ff.

430. *GB*, I, p. 384.

431. Pharmakos (Thargelia), Boulimos. Plutarch, *Quaestiones Convivales*, VI, 8, 1; Argei, at Rome (Marquardt, *op. cit.* n. 77 above, p. 191); Mannhardt, *MythForsch*, p. 135.

432. Cf. the Thargelia, expiation for the death of Androgeus. Gruppe, *Griechische Mythologie*, p. 37; the Karneia, that of Karnos, etc. Cf. legend of Melanippus and of Comaetho at Patras (Pausanias, VII, 19, 2ff).

CHAPTER FIVE

433. Mannhardt, *WFK*; *MythForsch*; Frazer, *GB*, I, pp. 213ff; II, pp. 1ff. Jevons, *Introduction to the History of Religion* (1896). Grant Allen, *Evolution of the Idea of God*, chap. x ff. Felix Liebrecht, 'Der aufgefressene Gott', in *Zur Volkskunde* (Heilbronn, 1879), pp. 436, 439. Goblet d'Alviella, 'Les Rites de la moisson', *Revue d'histoire des religions*, XXXVIII (1898), pp. 1ff. Robertson Smith, art. 'Sacrifice', *Encyclopedia Britannica*, 9th edn.; *RS*, pp. 414ff. Carl Vogt, 'Anthropophagie et sacrifices humains', *Compte-rendu du Congrès International d'Archéologie et Préhistoire*, Bologna, 1871 (Bologna, 1873), p. 325. We do not maintain that every sacrifice of the god is of agrarian origin.

434. Obviously we exclude the case of animal totems.

435. Mannhardt, *Korndämonen* (Berlin, 1868); *WFK*; *Myth Forsch*. Frazer, *GB*, II, the innumerable facts cited; the victim, the spirit of the fields, the last sheaf, all bear the same name. We follow their account here.

436. It even happens that eatables, etc., are placed there—a very elementary sacrifice. Mannhardt, *WFK*, I, p. 215.

437. Mannhardt, *WFK*, I, pp. 350, 363. Frazer, *GB*, I, pp. 381ff; II, pp. 21, 183ff. Porphyry, *De abstinentia*, II, 27.

438. Cf. Frazer, *GB*, I, p. 360.

439. Arnobius, *Adversus Natumes*, V, 5ff. (The legend of Agdistis, who obtains from Zeus a promise that the corpse of Attis will not rot.) Julian, *Oratio*, V, 180.

440. Philo of Byblos, 44.

441. Roscher, *Lexicon*, art. 'Ikarios'.

442. Chavero, *op. cit.* n. 133 above, p. 365.

443. Codex Ramirez: *Relacion del origen de los Indios*, ed. Vigil, p. 28. Bernardino de Sahagun, *Historia de las cosas de Nueva España*, II, 11 and 30.

444. H. H. Bancroft, *The Native Races of the Pacific States of North America* (New York, 1875–6), II, pp. 319ff. Frazer, *GB*, I, p. 221.
445. Firmicus Maternus, *De errore profanarum religionum*, 6. Rohde, *Psyche*, II, p. 166. Frazer, *Pausanias*, IV, p. 143.
446. Philo of Byblos (ed. Orelli), 34. Cf. perhaps *Bulletin de correspondance hellénique*, 1896, pp. 303ff. Inscription of El-Bardj: ἀποθεωθέντος ἐν τῷ λεβητι.
447. Mannhardt, *WFK*, II, p. 325.
448. In Lusatia the spirit who dwelt among the corn was called death. Frazer, *GB*, I, pp. 265ff. Cf. Mannhardt, *WFK*, I, p. 420. In other cases the birth of the spirit was enacted by giving the last sheaf and the first grains of corn the form of a child or a small animal (the *corn-baby* of English authors): the god was born from the agrarian sacrifice. See Mannhardt, *MythForsch*, pp. 6off. Frazer, *GB*, I, p. 344; II, pp. 23ff. Birth of the gods: of Zeus on Ida, and Gruppe, *Griechische Mythologie*, p. 248. Lydus, *De mensibus*, IV, 48. See Pausanias, VIII, 26, 6, for the birth of Athene at Aliphera and the cult of Zeus Λεχεάτης (giving birth). Soma is also very often called a young god, the youngest of the gods (like Agni). Bergaigne, *op. cit.* n. 131 above, I, p. 244.
449. Theopompus, fragm. 171 (*Fragm. Hist. Graec.*, I, p. 307). Pausanias, III, 13, 4. Oinomaus in Eusebius, *Praeparatio Evangelica*, V, 20, 3. Cf. H. Usener, 'Göttliche Synonyme', *Rheinisches Museum*, LIII (1898), pp. 359ff. Cf. for a legend of the same kind, *ibid.*, pp. 365ff.
450. See Hesychius, *s.v.*
451. Pausanias, III, 13, 3ff.
452. Lévi, *Sacrifice*, chap. II, cf. Bergaigne, *op. cit.* no. 131 above, I, pp. 101ff.
453. See Usener, *op. cit.* n. 398 above; *op. cit.* n. 449 above.
454. The mythical episodes are generally bound up with ritual ceremonies. Thus Cyprian relates that in his youth he had been a silent actor in the δράκοντος δραματουργία at Antioch (*Confessio S. Cypriani*, in *Acta Sanctorum*, Sept. 26, vol. VII Sept., p. 205). For the simulation of the fight of Apollo against Python at Delphi, see Frazer, *Pausanias*, III, p. 52; V, p. 244.
455. Cyril, *Adversus Julianum*, X, 342. Diodorus, VI, 5, 3.
456. Mannhardt, *WFK*, II, p. 133; cf. p. 149.
457. Clermont-Ganneau, 'La Stèle de Byblos', in *Bibliothèque de l'École des Hautes Études* (Paris), vol. XLIV (1880), p. 28. B. D. Eerdmans, 'Der Ursprung der Ceremonien des Hosein-Festes', in *Zeitschrift für Assyriologie*, IX (1894), pp. 28off.

458. E. J. Harper, 'Die Babylonischen Legenden von Etana, Zu, Adapa und Dibbarra', in Delitzsch, *Beiträge zur Assyriologie*, II. Cf. Eduard Stucken, *Astralmythen* (Leipzig, 1896–7), II, p. 89.

459. A. Jeremias, *Die Höllenfahrt der Ishtar* (cf. the purification of the carcase in the Vedic ritual, p. 41, n. 264).

460. Plutarch, *De Iside et Osiride*, sects. 13ff. Frazer, *GB*, I, pp. 301ff. Firmicus Maternus, *De errore profanarum religionum*, the burying of Osiris in the mysteries of Isis.

461. Pausanias, II, 32, 2.

462. A. Fournier, *Vieilles coutumes des Vosges*, p. 70.

463. Clement of Rome, *Recognitiones*, X, 24. Cf. Herodotus, VII, 167. F. C. Mövers, *Die Phönizier*, I, pp. 153, 155, 394ff. H. Pietschmann, *Geschichte der Phönizier* (1889). Smith, *RS*, p. 373, n. 2.

464. O. Müller, 'Sandon und Sardanapal', *Rheinisches Museum*, 1829, pp. 22–39.

465. Usener, *Götternamen* (Bonn, 1896), pp. 239ff.

466. See above, p. 79.

467. Plutarch, *Quaestiones Graecae*, 12.

468. Pausanias, IX, 34, 2.

469. And yet there are cases in which the three divine personages are killed in turn, as in the myth of Busiris and Lityerses (see Mannhardt, *MythForsch*, pp. 1ff); the stranger is killed by Busiris and Lityerses, these latter are killed by Herakles, and Herakles will commit suicide later.

470. Halévy, *Recherches bibliques* (Paris, 1895–1914), I, pp. 29ff. P. Jensen, *Die Kosmologie der Babylonier* (Strasbourg, 1890), pp. 263–364. Hermann Gunkel, *Schöpfung und Chaos in Urzeit und Endzeit* (1895); F. Delitzsch, *Das Babylonische Weltschöpfungsepos* (1896).

471. C. Clermont-Ganneau, 'Horus et Saint-Georges', *Revue archéologique*, N.S. XXXII (1876), pp. 196ff, 372ff; XXXIII (1877), 23; idem, 'La Stèle de Byblos', *Bibliothèque de l'École des Hautes-Études* (Paris), XLIV (1880), pp. 78–82.

472. Stengel, *GK*, pp. 101ff.

473. Festival of Zag-Mu-Ku (*resh-shatti*, beginning of the year). See O. E. Hagen, 'Keilschrifturkunden zur Geschichte des Königs Cyrus', *Beiträge zur Assyriologie*, II (1894), p. 238. *WAI,* IV, 23, 39ff. Cf. *Revue de philo.*, 1897, pp. 142ff.

474. Clermont-Ganneau, 'Horus et Saint-Georges' (see n. 471 above), p. 388.

475. Eusebius, *Chron.*, ed. Schone, I, 14, 18.

476. Cf. Hartland, *The Legend of Perseus*, III, for the myth of the sleeping hero and its equivalents. In the same way Indra falls exhausted after his struggle against the demon Vritra, or flees, etc. The same legend is related about Vishnu, etc.

477. Eudoxus, in Athenaeus, IX, 392E. Eustathius, *Iliad*, 1702, 50.

478. Hyginus, *Fabulae*, 80.

479. Usener, *Stoff der Griechischen Epos* (see n. 398 above).

480. K. 2801, 1 (*Beiträge zur Assyriologie*, III, p. 228; *ibid.*, II, pp. 258, 259). K. 2585. Somas judge of the Anunnaki. K 2606, Etana, murderer of the Anunnaki.

481. Cf. Talmud Babl., *Hullin*, 91b. T. Haarbrücker (trans.), *Abu-'l Fath' Muhammad ash-Shahrastani, Religionsparteien und Philosophenschulen* (Halle, 1850–1), vol. II, pp. 5ff.

482. Parthey, *Pap. Berl.*, I, v. 321ff.

483. Martianus Capella, *De nuptiis Philologiae et Mercurii*, II, 191.

484. *WAI*, IV, 21, 1c.

485. *WAI*, 14, 2. Rev. 9; Gibil, *mar apsi* (son of the abyss).

486. *WAI*, 22, 1. obv., 30.

487. Cf. Usener, 'Stoff der griechischen Epos', V. Thersites = Pharmakos accused by Achilles of having stolen the goblets of Apollo and put to death; and on the other hand Thersites = Theritas = Apollo.

488. Stucken, *Astralmythen*, II.

489. Oineus and the sons of Agrios. Usener, *op. cit.* n. 188 above, p. 375.

490. K. Tümpel, 'Der Karabos des Perseus', *Philologus*, LIII (N.F. VII), p. 544. Cf. Stucken, *Astralmythen*, I, pp. 233ff.

491. Porphyry, *De Antro nympharum*, 24. Darmesteter, *Ormazd et Ahriman*, pp. 327ff. It goes without saying that the symbolical explanations (e.g. in Gruppe, *Griechische Cultus und Mythologie*, pp. 153ff; Frazer, *GB*, I, p. 402) will not do. The symbol is only an explanation after the event both of the myth and the rite. Indeed, these legends are so naturally sacrificial that they can be replaced by episodes in which the god offers a sacrifice to himself: e.g., the legend of Perseus (Pausanias of Damascus, fragm. 3); Perseus offers a sacrifice to stop a flood (an introductory legend in the cycle, probably recent); legend of Aristaeus; Diodorus, IV, 81–2, Aristaeus sacrifices to stop a plague. Another legend, Virgil, *Georgics*, IV, 548ff. Cf. E. Maass, *Orpheus* (Munich, 1895), pp. 278–97; Gruppe, *Griechische Mythologie*, p. 249, n. 2;

Notes

Porphyry, *De antro nympharum*, 18). Cf. Samson's lion (Judg. xiv, 8). For the Mithraic sacrifice, see F. Cumont, *Textes et Monuments relatifs aux mystères de Mithra*, passim. Darmesteter, *Ormazd et Ahriman*, p. 150; for the sacrifying gods equivalent to the contestant gods, or rather struggling with the help of sacrifice, see Lévi, *Sacrifice*, II.

492. Mannhardt, *WFK*, I, p. 316.

493. *Adv. Julianum*, IV, 128.

494. L. Parmentier, 'Le Roi des Saturnales', *Revue de Philologie*, 1897, pp. 143ff.

495. e.g., *Athenische Mitteilungen*, XIII, 38, Pessinus.

496. Juan de Torquemada, *Monarchia Indiana* (Madrid, 1723), Bk. VI, chap. 38 (In Kingsborough, *Antiquities of Mexico* (London, 1830-48), VI, note, p. 414). Cortez, 3rd letter to Charles V (Kingsborough, VIII, note, p. 228).

497. Cf. Mannhardt, *WFK*, I, pp. 358ff; 572ff.

498. Proculus, Hymn to Athena, in Lobeck, *Aglaophamus* (Regensburg, 1829), I, p. 561; E. Abel, *Orphica* (Leipzig, 1885), p. 235.

499. See above, p. 82 (Karneia); see below, p. 90. Cf. Usener, *op. cit.* n. 188 above, p. 371.

500. See above, p. 79, n. 438.

501. Thus Herakles instituted the cult of Athena Αἰγοφάγος, after his fight with Hippocoon (Pausanias, III, 15, 9). After throwing the bulls of Geryon into the spring Kyane, he orders his action to be renewed (Diodorus, V, 4: 1-2).

502. Roscher, *Lexikon*, I, 1059; Frazer, *GB*, I, p. 328; cf. Hera, Αἰγοφαγος (Pausanias, III, 15, 9).

503. Frazer, *GB*, II, pp. 58ff. Cf. H. Seidel, 'System der Fetischverbote in Togo', *Globus*, LXXIII (1898), p, 355.

504. Frazer, *G.B.*, II, pp. 58ff. Cf. Diodorus, V, 62. Cf. the principle (Servius, *ad Aeneid.*, III, 18): *Victimae numinibus aut per similitudinem aut per contrarietatem immolabantur.*

505. A bibliography on Soma will be found in Macdonell, *Vedic Mythology* (Strasbourg, 1897), p. 115. See especially Bergaigne, *op. cit.* n. 131 above, I, 148, 125; II, 298, 366, etc. Hillebrandt, *op. cit.* n. 32 above, I (has a succinct account of the rite itself), pp. 146ff. On soma in the *Brahmanas*, see Lévi, *Sacrifice*, p. 169. The soma, an annual plant sacrificed in spring, seems to us to have been especially used originally in an agrarian rite. (See Bergaigne, *ibid.*, III, pp. 8 and 9, n. 1.) From the *RV* onwards, it is the 'king of plants' and classical India developed this theme: see Hillebrandt,

op. cit. III, p. 390. A complete study of the soma sacrifice has not yet been made. It will therefore be understood that we have not attempted to base anything on the texts, since the matter here is unlimited. As for naturalistic interpretations of the soma myth, we cannot discuss them, but we admit them all, not finding them in any respect incompatible.

506. Lévi, *Sacrifice*, p. 161. Bergaigne, *op. cit.* n. 131 above, III, pp. 84, 85, 63, n. 1, etc. Hillebrandt, *Viçvarapa*, p. 53, etc.

507. See Lévi, *Sacrifice*, chap. I and Preface.

508. Bergaigne, *op. cit.* n. 131 above, p. 275. See the remarkable discussion in Ludwig, *Rig-Veda*, III, p. 308.

509. Stucken, *Astralmythen*, II, p. 97. Talmud Babl., *Ta'anith*, Gemara, 27b. The world rests upon the sacrifice celebrated in the temple.

510. H. Gunkel, *Schöpfung und Chaos in Urzeit und Endzeit* (Göttingen, 1895).

511. See Vogt, *op. cit.* n. 433, p. 325. Cf. Lasaulx, *Die Sühnopfer der Griechen* (1841).

CHAPTER SIX

512. H. Callaway, *Religious System of the Amazulu*, p. 59, cf. p. 92.

INDEX

Numbers in italics refer to notes (by note number, not by page)

53022174R00098

Made in the USA
Columbia, SC
10 March 2019